NORTHERN OHIO
COLD CASES

JANE ANN TURZILLO

THE
History
PRESS

Published by The History Press
Charleston, SC
www.historypress.com

First published 2024

Manufactured in the United States

ISBN 9781467154376

Library of Congress Control Number: 2023946771

For John-Paul, Nick and Nathan, with all my love

Murder may pass unpunished for a time,
But tardy justice will o'ertake the crime.
—John Dryden

CONTENTS

ACKNOWLEDGEMENTS

This is the fourth book that I have had the pleasure of working with John Rodrigue as my editor. He has always been just an email and a few minutes away. My beta reader, Marilyn Seguin, deserves a special thanks for reading my manuscript and making sure it all made sense and was error free.

I was honored to be able to interview some of the victims' family and friends. Nancy Martins Baer and Steve Martins are Judy Martins's sister and brother. Edith Metz and Mark Metz are Frank Noch's daughter and grandson. Sheryl Eagleson Garza is Nancy Eagleson's sister, and Jeanne Windsor is the spokesperson for the Eagleson family. Mandi Dipple and Paul Dipple are the granddaughter and son-in-law of Police Chief Robert Hamrick. Ellen Lane is the former receptionist of the Lee Turzillo Contracting Company, and Garry Cowden was a long-time employee in difference capacities. Without these folks, I could not have come to know their lost loved ones and friends. These folks were the backbone of my research.

Law enforcement was a huge help in my research. Chief David P. Centner, Hinckley Police Department, gave me information and allowed me to take photos for the chapter on Police Chief Mel Wiley; Detective Eric Costante, Sandusky Police Department, supplied me with the file on Jane Doe/Patricia Greenwood; U.S. Marshal Pete Elliott, Northern District of Ohio, was generous with his time in helping me with information on Patricia Greenwood and Judy Martins; Latrice Evans, Records Clerk, Richmond Heights Police Department, located the Frank Noch file and sent it to me; Sheriff Jason K. Landers, Paulding County, shared information on Nancy

Eagleson's murder case; Sheriff Paul Sigsworth, Erie County, provided me with information and the initial sheriff's report on the Cassidy murder case; and Lieutenant Sean Ward, Ashtabula County Sheriff's Department, copied the thick file on Police Chief Robert Hamrick and photos for me. Many thanks for all their help.

Librarians are some of my favorite people. Those who have helped with my research are Rebecca Larson-Troyer, librarian, Special Collections Division, Akron–Summit County Public Library; Mary Plazo, manager, Special Collections Division, Akron–Summit County Public Library; Carrie Wimer, Local History/Genealogy/Archive, Ashtabula Public Library; Stewart Gibbs, business librarian, The Public Library of Youngstown and Mahoning County; Lisa Rienerth, librarian, Medina County Library; and as always, thanks to Brian Meggitt, CPL photo collection.

Emma Schute, Hinkley Township Historical Society; Susan Hill, Ashtabula County Historical Society; Jayne Davis, researcher; and Richard Dana Esq. were most helpful during my research.

Journalists Brian Dugger, WTOL; Mark Price, *Akron Beacon Journal*; and Ted Wendling, former *Plain Dealer* reporter, helped me hunt down resources.

Others who dug in their files to find valuable pieces of information or photos were Ryan Colby, court administrator, Eastern Ashtabula County Court; Kevin Guimette, communications coordinator, City of Green; Tom Horsman, communications manager, City Manager's Office, the City of Sandusky; Laura Kennedy, Medina County Probate; Sandy Keovisay, case manager, Cuyahoga County Medical Examiner's Office; and Kyle L. Walker.

I always thank fellow writer and researcher Wendy Koile, my brainstorming group of Julie Anne Lindsey, Kathryn Long, Cari Dubiel, Wendy Campbell, Shellie Arnold, Laura Critchfield and Danielle Haas. Thank you to the Northeast Ohio Sisters in Crime.

And a huge thanks to my family. I can always count on them for support.

INTRODUCTION

The idea for this book took root in October 1980 with the brutal slaying of Norman L. Liver Jr. He was a man I had known and respected throughout most of my life. He was the executive vice president and a valuable part of my father's company. When he did not come into the office one day, his co-workers had his Lakewood apartment building's manager do a welfare check. His body was found when the manager opened the door. His senseless murder has never been solved.

It got me thinking about other cold cases—long before Netflix, Amazon Prime and shows like *Unsolved Mysteries* put them on our TVs and before all of today's wonderful podcasts helped us through our morning workouts and drives to and from work.

I started reading true crime books by Ann Rule and others to learn how they handled homicide, and I began saving newspaper clippings about other unsolved cases. After all these years, I have a number of folders crammed into my file cabinet. Some of the files are fat with yellowed, brittle clippings from all over Ohio. Some of the cases have already shown up in my 2015 book *Unsolved Murders & Disappearances in Northeast Ohio.*

I selected eleven more cases for this book by first deciding I wanted to cover northern Ohio. Next, I looked at the victims. After all, unsolved murders are really about the victims and the people who loved them.

Judy Martins was a beautiful Kent State University coed who disappeared off the campus after a dorm party. She was a compassionate young woman and thought she might like to become a counselor. She loved her family dearly.

Frank Noch came to the United States from Germany as a young man. He was a mathematical genius and valuable employee at the General Motors plant in Cleveland. In addition to being inventive, he was creative and made mobiles for hospitals. Someone broke into his home, bound, gagged and killed him. His daughter found him.

Hinckley police chief Mel Wiley had a secret. Maybe that is why he disappeared. Before he joined the ranks of the missing, he lay crumbs to lead his friends to think he had drowned in Lake Erie.

DNA helped Sandusky Police identify a Jane Doe forty-three years to the day after she washed up on the shores of Lake Erie. Now, detectives are hoping to solve who put Patricia Greenwood in the water and why.

Fourteen-year-old Nancy Eagleson and her five-year-old sister, Sheryl, had a fun day at the movies. But as they walked toward their Paulding home, a man drove up, grabbed Nancy and shoved her into his car. Sheryl tried to stop him, but she was no match for the abductor. Nancy was found in a field several hours later.

Marion Brubaker was riding her bike home from the Portage Lakes Library through a wooded shortcut when she was attacked and strangled. The twelve-year-old was a minister's daughter who loved music and books.

John and Shelly Markley went missing from their Bristolville home ten days before Christmas in 1995. They left five children, ages eight through fifteen, behind. The couple were last seen at the drive-up window of their bank. They withdrew $1,000 from their savings account and were accompanied by a stranger, the teller said.

The early-morning triple slaying of the Cassidy family in Erie County's Milan has never been solved. William and Ann were shot in their bed with their own shotgun. Their daughter Patricia, twelve, was bludgeoned. The gun was never found, and neither was the person who used it.

Steve's Motel in Summit County had an unsavory reputation for a number of reasons, including illicit sex, drugs, overdoses and more. But the worst was the gruesome murders of the owners, Maher and Jyoti Patel, and their six-year-old daughter, Alka.

Rock Creek police chief Robert Hamrick was fatally injured during a high-speed chase in 1970. For years, theories have swirled around how he died. Did he die from injuries suffered in the accident? Or did an unknown person(s) deal the final blows after his cruiser crashed?

If you know anything that might help law enforcement solve any of these crimes, please, please call the proper agency.

1

WHERE DID HINCKLEY POLICE CHIEF MEL WILEY GO?

F riday, July 26, 1985, started out like any other morning for Hinckley Township police chief Mel Wiley. He made his early stop at the K & K Donuts before heading into work in the 150-year-old house that served as the township police station. He ordered his usual cup of coffee with cream and puffed on a Salem Menthol while he sat and drank it. The hefty, 5'11", 195-pound Wiley always looked the same. He wore his graying hair in a self-chopped buzz cut that hid his receding hairline. His uniform had a few wrinkles and some cat hair clinging to the dark fabric. Like every other morning, he cracked his usual corny jokes while talking with folks in the shop and teased owners Mary Kirby and Carol Kosman about their donuts. Everything was normal—or so it appeared.

Hinkley Township is best known for buzzards. It rests in the northeast corner of Medina County in northeast Ohio. Forty-seven-year-old Melvin Lee Wiley seemed like the ideal police chief for the quiet, mostly crime-free township. He was a former Medina County sheriff's deputy, army intelligence officer, FBI fingerprint clerk and investigator for the U.S. Department of Defense. He attended Brigham Young University and George Washington University in D.C. He was somewhat odd, not neatly pressed and polished like most officers, but he was a good cop, a deep thinker, level-headed and stable.

But then he vanished.

The mystery of Wiley's disappearance began on Tuesday, July 30, 1985, at 4:00 a.m. when an Ohio Department of Natural Resources park ranger

Hinckley Township police chief Mel Wiley went missing in July 1985 and has not been seen since. *From the* Akron Beacon Journal, *USA Today Network.*

reported an abandoned 1980 Toyota Corolla station wagon at Edgewater Park in Cleveland, not far from the Amtrack station. Rangers had been keeping an eye on the locked-up tan-colored car since the night before, park assistant manager Jim Frabotta told reporters at the time.

By later in the day, no one had showed up to drive the vehicle away, so park rangers opened it. Inside, they found a pair of blue pants, a blue shirt, blue socks and a towel, all neatly folded. Stacked on top of the clothing were a black belt, brown shoes, two packs of Salem Menthol cigarettes, keys, a bottle of suntan lotion, a watch and a Hinckley, Ohio police chief's badge. A wallet containing a driver's license belonging to Melvin L. Wiley with a

Mel Wiley started out every morning at K & K Donuts before going into the police station. *Hinckley Historical Society.*

Hinckley Township Police Department in 1985. *Hinckley Historical Society.*

birthdate of May 6, 1938, and a Hinckley Township Police identification card were found in the glove compartment, along with credit cards and $15.77 in folding money and coins. Other than that, nothing seemed to be out of place. There was no blood on the seats, the steering wheel or even the clothing. There were no signs of foul play. The only oddity that Hinckley's former police chief Len Keller noted was the driver's seat had been moved forward, as if a shorter person had been driving it.

The rangers contacted the Hinckley Township Police Department and learned the chief had not been in the office since the previous Friday and had not called in sick. Surprisingly, no one had questioned his absence. In turn, Hinckley police notified Medina City police, where Wiley lived.

Medina detective James R. Bigam got the call. He and Wiley had been long-time friends, dating back to their days as deputies on the Medina County Sheriff's Department.

While park authorities dragged Lake Erie and scoured the beach in search of the missing chief, Bigam, along with Hinckley dispatcher Virginia Yates, set out for Wiley's apartment. The door was locked, but they gained entrance through an open window. Nothing seemed to be disturbed inside,

Park authorities dragged Lake Erie and scoured Edgewater Park's beach in search of Mel Wiley. *Cleveland Public Library Photo Collection.*

but the apartment was unusually clean and tidy. The refrigerator was even emptied out except for a jar of mayonnaise. Bigam had never known his friend to be that neat.

Several days' worth of food and water had been left for his three cats. Wiley was very attached to his cats and treated them like children.

As Bigam looked around the apartment, he became aware of what was missing. Wiley had been writing a mystery titled *Harvest of Madness*, a police procedural set in Burnt Cabins, Pennsylvania. Everyone knew about the chief's novel. He talked about it all the time. He loved writing and belonged to a Medina writers' group. When he first came to Medina, he had worked as a staff writer at the *Medina Gazette*. He continued to write a nostalgia column titled "Glimpses of Yesteryear" for the *Hinckley Reporter* after he became chief. His dream was to be the next Joseph Wambaugh, so *Harvest of Madness* was always close at hand in case inspiration struck. Bigam searched the apartment for the manuscript, but it was not in there. That meant it was wherever Wiley was.

Wiley also wrote poetry and would read his poems to anyone who would listen. While he was a deputy in the sheriff's department, he wrote *My Love Is a Silver Shadow*, a book of which he was very proud. That book was not in the apartment, either.

Wiley also liked music and had thought he would make a good disc jockey. His music tapes were not in the apartment. His address book and a scrapbook were also missing.

A note was left on the kitchen table as a reminder to pick up his uniforms from the dry cleaners. Bigam found this strange. He had never known his friend to have his uniforms dry-cleaned or pressed.

Detective Bigam drove to the dry cleaners where Wiley's uniforms were waiting to be picked up. The person behind the counter handed the detective an envelope that had been fished out of one of the uniform pockets. Bigam opened it and found a Yellow Cab schedule and a Greyhound Bus schedule from Cleveland to Fort Ord in California. Wiley had been stationed at Fort Ord near San Francisco part of the time while he was in the army. The date "July 28" was penciled on the schedule in Wiley's handwriting.

As for the station wagon, Wiley loved it. He had inherited it from his brother, Clark, who died of cancer two years earlier. He had taken his brother's death hard, so for him to abandon it did not make sense to Bigam. He loved that car. And yet, the cab and bus schedules, the condition of Wiley's apartment and the missing manuscripts led Bigam to consider his friend had planned to leave everything behind and disappear.

Mel Wiley's 1980 station wagon was found abandoned at Edgewater Park in Cleveland on July 30, 1985, at 4:00 a.m. *Author's collection.*

In the meantime, park authorities found nothing to suggest Chief Wiley had been in the water or that he had been anywhere near the beach. Searchers said if he had drowned, his body would likely surface in the warm waters within a matter of a few days and possibly wash ashore. Frabotta told reporters the possibility of Wiley's body being out in the lake was "extremely remote."

Judy Easter, a woman Wiley had been dating for five months, was the last person to see or talk to him. The exchange was on the Saturday before he disappeared. He told her he planned to go swimming with an out-of-town friend at Edgewater Park on Sunday. He never mentioned the friend's name but did say he needed to buy a pair of swim trunks. She thought that was strange, because she had tried to get him to go swimming with her at Findley State Park, but he was not interested.

When Wiley saw her later Saturday evening, he said he tried to buy a pair of swim trunks at Kmart, but the cashier told him if he waited a day, swimwear would be half off on a blue-light special, so he was going to wait to buy it at the reduced price. She and Wiley then planned a date for Monday. He left her house at around midnight. That was the last she saw of him. When he did not turn up for their Monday date, she tried calling him, but he did not answer the phone. It was unlike him to break a date. He always kept his word, she said.

Detectives spoke with Kmart's manager and found out there was no blue-light special on swimwear. In fact, the store had sent swimwear back to the main warehouse in the middle of July.

The idea of Wiley going swimming did not seem plausible to those who knew him. Nancy Abbott, a Hinckley Township trustee at the time, told reporters that "Mel didn't like the sun. He had fair skin."

When talking to area newspapers, Bigam said, "Also, he had radiation scars and marks on his body and he wouldn't be one to be displaying all that." Wiley always wore long sleeves to cover spots, even in the hottest months. The patches of pale skin were on his neck and arms. His mother, Doris Wiley, explained he had suffered the scarring from an accident during his time at the Nevada Atomic Test Site while in the army.

Investigators' next contact was Wiley's former wife, Cynthia Manzer. The couple were married for seventeen years. "Cindy" moved to New York and took her maiden name back after their November 1983 divorce. She told Bigam there was no way her ex would go swimming because of his radiation burns. According to an October 1985 article in *Ohio Magazine* by Bob McKay, she suggested that he "ran away" to Chinatown in San Francisco, because he loved everything about it, from the writings to the music to the art. It was "his Mecca," she said.

In later years, Cindy shared that he came up missing one other time. It was before they were married, and he was to be the best man at a friend's wedding. He was gone for four or five days.

At the Hinckley Township police station, Bigam and Sergeant David Yates (dispatcher Virginia's husband) opened Wiley's top desk drawer. It was usually hard to pull out for the jumble of odds and ends, but this time it slid out easily and was empty except for a key to his apartment. They figured it was left to be found so someone would go to his cats.

Over the years, Wiley had collected model trains. They were still displayed in the office on the loop of tracks he built for his collection. Trains were one of his favorite hobbies. Michelle Short wrote on CrimeWire that Wiley's father was an engineer for the Baltimore & Ohio Railroad. His mother told detectives he loved trains because he grew up near the AC&Y railroad tracks in Lorain, where his family lived. As an adult, he traveled to Pittsburgh on occasion so he could ride one of the old steam engines back to Medina. It is interesting that a train schedule also turned up during the investigation, and it was noted the Amtrack train station was a mere one hundred yards from where Wiley's car had been found.

In talking with the Yateses, Bigam learned of Wiley's other "hobby," which had nothing to do with trains.

Virginia explained that she thought Wiley had been acting suspicious. She suspected he was not always using his typewriter for police business. According to *Plain Dealer* reporter Ted Wendling's July 28, 1991 article, "Seamy untold story surfaces in Hinckley chief's disappearance," she said Wiley would cover up whatever he was working on when she entered his office. His actions made her curious, so she quietly started rummaging around in his wastebasket. According to police records that Wendling saw in 1991, Virginia retrieved at least two hundred pages of pornography and pornographic writings in 1983. Included were obscene drawings and drafts of long letters pouring out his love to a married woman known as "Nancy Morgan."

Police Chief Wiley had written fictional stories describing explicit sexual acts with some of the female members of St. Paul Episcopal Church in Medina. He did not attend the church, but Cindy had been a member of the choir and was friends with some of the women in the stories. A June 18, 2000 *Akron Beacon Journal* article, "Missing police chief leaves unsolved mystery," by Carol Biliczky reported that Wiley's marriage to Cindy ended because of his fondness of pornography. Wiley was devastated by the divorce, even though he was having an affair.

Along with Wiley's pornographic writings, Virginia found a signed order form for twenty-eight dollars' worth of stories about incest from a San Diego publisher. Whether Wiley actually ordered the materials was never known.

According to Wendling's article, the Yateses failed to note their findings in the reports they filed when Wiley disappeared because they felt it was "inappropriate for the information to be disseminated to the public."

Wendling's article included a photo of a police report that revealed that Wiley had been writing "dirty stories" for some time and that some of the subjects included the church ladies' names, addresses and phone numbers. Bigam never interviewed any of them, because he "didn't think I had enough in that area and it wasn't going to solve the disappearance." He said, "it only showed that Wiley had 'fantasies.'" The church rector also called the stories "fantasies."

The ribbon in Wylie's typewriter came the closest to making sense of his disappearance. Because the ribbon was intended to be used only one time, detectives were able to re-create several drafts of a long farewell letter he wrote to "Nancy Morgan." Their affair started before his divorce from Cindy and continued until March 1985. Wiley opened a post office box for her, and their affair was carried out mostly through the mail. He poured his heart out in love letters to her.

But the woman ended the affair, telling Wiley she was never going to leave her husband, who had been ill for some time. She told him that even if she were single, she would not marry him.

A Medina police report, seen by Wendling, disclosed that one of Hinckley's patrolmen wrote a letter to Wiley threatening to reveal his affair with the married Medina woman to the trustees and newspapers. The threat was never fully investigated, and no one questioned the officer who allegedly wrote the letter.

According to McKay's article, Bigam knew the woman because she worked in the sheriff's department, and he suspected his friend Wiley had strong feelings for her.

The woman told investigators she had cashed in a $2,000 insurance policy and loaned him the money. Whatever he needed it for, he never paid it back. Instead, he named her as the beneficiary of some small retirement policies. She and Wiley also entered into an arrangement where she would type up his manuscript, and they would split the profits when it sold.

From what detectives could decipher of the letter off the typewriter ribbon, Wiley was clearly obsessed with the woman. It read in part: "A couple of nights ago, long after dark, when I felt no one in particular, you included, might see me…I took a walk that eventually led me down your street and past you house." He said he realized they could never be together, but he would retain happy memories of their time.

> *In three or four months, you've taken a man and have given him some of the major things he's pretty much desperately wanted most of his life—love; affection; a sense of real purpose for someone who counts a great deal to him, a sense of being worthwhile after all, and lastly a realization that you, for one, pretty much like him and want him for the person he happens to be. If that isn't leaving a "mark" by you, of some kind, I certainly don't know what it is. True, it's only one item, but don't you think what you've done there that makes up for possible numbers if you were inclined to keep a running score? Quality. Not quantity.*

The letter revealed that he felt his life was going nowhere and that nothing ever worked out for him. He stressed that he wanted to write, and that's where he found the most satisfaction. "I think that's what I was 'made' for." He added that he was beginning to feel burned out from police work.

He disclosed that by the time she got the letter he would be 2,500 miles from Medina, but he indicated a possibility of making secret visits back to see how the area changed. "I will have, in one sense of the word, gone away. It's a one-way trip, so I'm told with no option of ever returning and perhaps that's just as well for any and all concerned." The letter continued, "Try not to judge me too harshly. I'm not trying to hurt anyone and if I do, that was not my intention. Right or wrong, I'm just doing what I think is the best solution for me."

The name Tod Allan Moran with a birthdate and Social Security number was typed at the end of one of the drafts. A search for that name, date and Social Security number went nowhere. Tod Allan Moran was the name of the protagonist in *Harvest of Madness*,

Detective Bigam held a press conference where he told reporters about the letter. "We now feel we can prove that Mel is alive." He said the typewriter ribbon gave some insight to Wiley's mindset and feelings at the time. In more than one interview with the media, Bigam said he felt he knew his friend Wiley better than Wiley knew himself.

"Nancy Morgan" claimed she never received the letter, but two days after Wiley's disappearance, she closed the post office box.

Bigam apparently believed she had not received the letter. He told the *Chicago Tribune*, "He probably realized at the last minute that if he sent the letter, it would probably give away his plans." On the other hand, perhaps Wiley felt guilty, maybe embarrassed of his feelings, and he destroyed the letter, Bigam said.

Hinckley Township trustees kept Mel Wiley on the roster as their chief of police until September 30 in case he returned. After that, they declared the $23,500-a-year job to be opened to new applicants. Ultimately, they chose David Yates, who had been serving as interim chief, and gave him a one-year contract in January 1986.

A few years after Wiley's disappearance, his sister Myra Kirkle hired Robert M. Arsiaga, a Kansas City, Missouri private investigator. Although Arsiaga visited Medina and tried to unravel what may have happened to Wiley, he came up empty-handed.

The family tossed around the theory that he was being blackmailed and that is why he left. That idea did not go very far with Bigam. "I don't think he was blackmailed. I think he pretty much got fed up with where his life was at." Although he was as far up in rank as he could get, he was not satisfied, the detective said.

Left: Hinckley Township police chief Mel Wiley's badge. He disappeared on July 28, 1985. *Badge courtesy of Hinckley Township Police, photo by Jane Ann Turzillo.*

Below: Hinckley Township police chief Mel Wiley's handcuffs. "Mel" is engraved into both cuffs. *Handcuffs courtesy of Hinckley Township Police, photo by Jane Ann Turzillo.*

The last time Doris Wiley saw her son was on June 7, 1985, according to a November 1993 *Akron Beacon Journal* article by staff writer William Canterbury. She spoke with him on July 24, 1985: "a brief call to him at his job and asked him to stop at the house," she said. He could have retired in a few years, Mrs. Wiley told *Plain Dealer* reporter Terry Holthaus. She never accepted the notion that her son ran away.

In January 1985, Medina County probate judge L. Thomas Skidmore appointed Doris Wiley the trustee for her son's estate. In November 1993, Skidmore pronounced Wiley "presumed dead for estate purposes." Mrs.

Wiley was the only person to testify at a hearing to legally close Melvin L. Wiley's estate. Canterbury's article referenced a claim for unpaid alimony of $1,790 plus interest owed to Cynthia Manzer Northrup.

Wiley did not leave a will, but he had two state employee retirement accounts. Although "Nancy Morgan" had signed an agreement with Wiley in 1984, naming her as sole beneficiary, both retirement accounts went to his mother. The case file #48466 showed his assets were less than $5,000.

Wiley's sister Karen passed away in February 1993. His mother, Doris, died in June 1995. His sister Myra has not answered inquiries. Detective Bigam died in 2016.

So, what happened to Police Chief Mel Wiley? If he's still alive, he may still be writing mystery novels. He may even belong to a writers' club. He might be found down by the steel ribbon tracks, watching the trains thunder by, or he may belong to a model train club.

We will probably never know the truth. The evidence is gone, and the Medina City police say they have no file on him.

The arrows kept pointing to San Francisco, but he had connections in Florida, too. Wherever Wiley went, Bigam was convinced that he had "walked off into the sunset in the truest sense."

2

STEVE'S NO-TELL MOTEL

T hings seemed off to Bonnie (not her real name), the day clerk at the infamous Steve's Motel in Green, a village between Akron and Canton, when she arrived at work at 7:00 a.m. on Monday, October 22, 1991. It was strange that the owner had not shown up at the office with the cash box. She grew even more concerned by 8:00 a.m. when her boss's daughter failed to emerge from the adjacent house to catch the school bus. Wondering if the child might be sick, she decided to check.

She walked the short distance from the office over to the brick Cape Cod–style house. The door was ajar. She knocked and called out. No answer came. So, she pushed the door farther open and stepped into a horrific scene. Sprawled on the floor in the living room by the coffee table was the owner, Manher T. Patel, thirty-nine. His wife, Jyoti, thirty-two, was lying between the kitchen and dining area. Both had been shot in the head. Upstairs, their six-year-old daughter, Alka, had also been shot in the head while she slept in her bed. She was only a first grader at Greenwood Elementary School.

According to the October 22 and 23, 1991 *Canton Repository* articles by Jan H. Kennedy ("Motel Owners, Daughter Shot to Death in Green") and Dave Sereno ("Authorities Searching for the Leads in Green Triple Homicide"), Summit County sheriff's detectives figured the motive was robbery at first, but they did not rule out revenge or the possibility that the victims knew their killer. There were no signs of forced entry, but the motel's cash box was empty, and coins were scattered on the living room floor. Drawers in

Street view of Steve's Motel in Green, Summit County. *Photo by Kevin Guilmette, Communications Coordinator, City of Green.*

an upstairs bedroom had been riffled. Later, detectives found a briefcase containing $2,000.

Reporter Kennedy wrote that Sergeant Eugene Scott estimated that the family was killed sometime during the night. Sheriff David Troutman told Sereno the murder of the whole family "looked to be execution style."

Well known as a spot for illicit affairs and hookups, the property consisted of twenty reddish-brown cabins, the office and the house, which sat near the entrance of the nearly three-acre parcel. The cabins could be rented by the hour or for a whole night for fifteen dollars. Each cabin was named for a famous gangster—Al Capone, John Dillinger, Pretty Boy Floyd, Baby Face Nelson. Cabin no. 13 had carpeting on the walls to cut down on the noise. It was a favorite of the repeat clientele. The clerk at the office also offered condoms.

Detectives knew the investigation was going to be tough because of the establishment's reputation as a "no-tell motel." And the Patels did not keep a registry. Guests did not even need to get out of the car to pay and check in; however, the clerk on duty would regularly write down license plate numbers.

Sunday nights were often slow, so there was no overnight clerk on October 20 to note license plates. However, detectives learned that a small red car bearing Georgia plates was seen leaving the motel early Monday morning. The owner of that car later contacted the sheriff's department, having heard about the murders through the media. After talking with the car's owner, detectives dismissed the person as a suspect.

Investigators believed only three couples had rented cabins that night. Captain William E. Lewis, commander of the sheriff's department detective bureau at that time, told the *Akron Beacon Journal*'s staff writer Robert Hoiles, "We're still investigating every lead we have." Detectives were able to track down and rule out the involvement of everyone who stayed at the motel that Sunday night or early Monday morning. Lewis would not reveal what they had learned from any of those clients.

Ohio Bureau of Investigation technicians scoured the entire property and buildings for forensic evidence and clues. Sheriff's detectives interviewed family members, friends, neighbors, employees and any clientele who came forward.

Steve's Motel was originally built by Yugoslavian immigrants Stephen and Mary Durgala as a "tourist camp" of twenty cabins in the mid-1930s. The adjacent house was built at the same time. The motel opened for business in 1937. Interstate 77 had not been built yet, but the traffic from Routes 619 and 241 provided a steady stream of lodgers. The couple also rented out the cabins to laborers who came to Akron looking for work in the rubber shops. It was a reputable business back then.

In addition to caring for her and her husband's eight children, Mary cleaned the cabins and served meals to the guests. Upon request, she would wash their clothes, using an old-fashioned washboard and tub.

When Stephen died in 1954, the property passed to Mary. In the next few years, she sold off pieces of the land to family and others.

Steve's Motel fell into the hands of Steve Alan Kelly in the late 1950s. Under his ownership, it was transformed into an adults-only destination that switched from weekly to hourly rentals. Kelly painted the cabins red and kept them clean and sanitized. Each cabin came with a double bed, a sink and toilet. The décor featured red lights on the ceilings and mirrors on the walls. Kelly was the first to name the cabins for gangsters and carpet Cabin no. 13's walls. A sign, "Notorious Steve's Motel," stood along Route 619 to warn traveling families to keep driving. A sign out front boasted "free air conditioning." Later, Kelly added "free movies" (porno) and "hot tubs" to the sign. Customers, who had to be at least eighteen, could rent by the hour, but no more than two people were permitted in a cabin at one time.

Steve's Motel did a good business with repeat customers. At any particular time, cars belonging to prominent citizens would be parked in the lot outside

Manher T. Patel; his wife, Jyoti; and their six-year-old daughter were murdered in this house, adjacent to the office. *Photo by Kevin Guilmette, Communications Coordinator, City of Green.*

Each cabin was named for a famous gangster. *Photo by Kevin Guilmette, Communications Coordinator, City of Green.*

a cabin. Occasionally, an angry wife would show up and cause a scene upon finding a philandering spouse.

Manher T. Patel bought the motel from Kelly on a twenty-year-land contract. He put $125,000 down and owed $400,000. The papers were filed October 13, 1989.

Manher was born in India and had lived on a farm two hundred miles north of Bombay. He came to the United States about 1977 looking to be financially successful. According to the family's obituary in the *Akron Beacon Journal,* Jyoti came to the United States from the Fiji islands a year later. The couple lived in Chicago, where their daughter, Alka, was born, and where Manher worked as a press operator at a tool-and-die shop. He wanted to be his own boss, and Steve's Motel with a house on-site was the perfect opportunity. The Patels added disco balls and waterbeds to the cabins. A sign hanging outside the motel read "American ownership."

Although they followed Indian customs of Manher wearing a turban and Jyoti often wearing a sari, they were proud to become American citizens. Both had studied English at the Portage Lakes Career Center for two years, and they worked hard to be fluent.

Other Indian families owned and ran motels in the Akron-Canton area. Manher's brother Kanu said the motel business was easy for foreigners to run, and it was a way for families to live and work together. Their sister and brother-in-law Jita and Dipak Patel owned the Office Motel not far away. Several Indian families shared the surname Patel because it is a caste name and a way to identify families.

After the murders, Kanu T. Patel took over the motel, but in December 1994, he ran into his own trouble. He caught David B. Wheele, a part-time clerk at Steve's Motel, drinking on the job and allegedly beat the man so severely with a 5 iron golf club that the imprint of the club head could be seen on Wheele's back. Wheele died three days later from a blood clot as a result of the beating. Kanu was tried for involuntary manslaughter, but the trial ended in a hung jury and he was not retried.

A few weeks after the triple slayings, the Patel family offered a $5,000 reward for information leading to the arrest and conviction of the killer, but the promise of money brought no new clues. After ten months of no tips, the Patel family raised the reward to $12,000. Sheriff's Lieutenant Larry Momchilov told *Akron Beacon Journal* staff writer Robert Hoiles ("More Money Offered for Family's Killer") that detectives were following up on any lead, but helpful information was not coming in very fast.

After hundreds of interviews and thousands of hours of combing through the evidence, investigators were still stumped. Several sets of eyes had gone over the case, but it was still not solved. Questions remained. If it was robbery, why take the cash box and leave a briefcase with $2,000 behind? Why rob the place on a Sunday night—the slowest night of the week? And why kill the child upstairs? Could it have been a hate crime? Were ethnic gangs involved? Or was it a contract hit?

After thirty years, detectives came up with a theory to answer those questions. The sheriff's department would not share the case file, alleging that "no documents are being released for this as it is still on-going investigation." Instead, they pointed to a December 16, 2021 *Akron Beacon Journal* web edition article, "A Hired Hit, a Flying Robber, and 3 Murders," written by Stephanie Warsmith and Paula Schleis, in which Captain (now Major) Scott Cottle, commander of the sheriff's department detective bureau, said, "It was a business dealing that went south. Some kind of business dealing that triggered the response of a professional hit man coming in—and leaving town right away."

Detectives theorized someone was hired to kill the family because Green was on the verge of becoming a city in 1991. Property values began to explode, and that corner was a prime piece of land for development.

A view of Steve's Motel cabins with the office at left. *Photo by Kevin Guilmette, Communications Coordinator, City of Green.*

Office of Steve's Motel with ragged flag. *Photo by Kevin Guilmette, Communications Coordinator, City of Green.*

Years after the slayings, detectives revealed that at the time of the murder, an informant told an Akron police detective that Akron-born bank robber Frank Lawrence Sprenz and Irish mobster James "Whitey" Bulger were connected to the Patel "hit," but at that time, there was no evidence to back up that information.

Then, eight years after the murders, Sprenz—aka the "Flying Bank Robber" for fleeing his crimes in stolen airplanes—wanted to talk to detectives from his Columbus prison cell where he was doing twenty-five to fifty. He contacted sheriff's detectives and told them a story of how he was involved in the Patel "hit." This fit the information the Akron detective heard at the time of the murders. Sprenz wanted to trade "specific facts" for leniency. The detectives were interested, but when they drove down to Columbus to meet with him, he clammed up.

Sprenz died in 2016, just two months after he was denied parole, and Bulger was murdered in a West Virginia prison in October 2018. Their deaths left sheriff's detectives with no definite proof to connect the two with the murders.

Through the years, the motel earned the nickname "Sleazy Steve's" and was a trouble spot for the safety forces. The front office was robbed several times, and in 1971, the night clerk shot and killed a twenty-eight-year-old would-be robber. The sheriff's department investigated everything from a kidnapping to domestic violence. There were drug overdoses, some of them fatal. Drug busts were a regular occurrence, including the collar of a major cocaine supplier. Suicides, drunken assaults and other illegal activities kept the sheriff's department and medics busy. According to the *Akron Beacon Journal*, deputies were called to the motel 363 times between 2015 and 2020. Medics were called 48 times over that same period.

The property and motel changed owners six times over the next fifteen years after the Patels' deaths. Little was done in the way of maintenance. The cabins, office and house had deteriorated. The whole property was run down, and taxes were delinquent.

The City of Green purchased the property for approximately $190,000 in the spring of 2021. The notorious Steve's Motel met with the wrecking ball soon after.

3

THE BRUTAL MURDER OF
FRANK NOCH

Frank Noch was an eighty-six-year-old German immigrant and a World War I German army veteran. He could not drive anymore, but that did not stop him from getting places. Although he was getting up in age, he was in fine shape and walked wherever he wanted to go.

"He wanted to stay active and healthy," Edie Metz said of her father. She recalled how he would walk from his home in Richmond Heights to Euclid Beach because he wanted to join his friends at a retirement get-together. He had friends who lived in a senior apartment building in Euclid Beach, so he walked there often to visit.

Neighbors knew him to walk at least five miles every day, but the last time they saw him alive was on February 20, 1984, about 4:00 p.m. He was walking toward his home on Beverley Hills Drive just off Chardon Road. Sometime within the next hour and forty-five minutes, Frank Noch was murdered.

Frank was a widower who lived alone in his brick two-story house. His daughters, Rosemarie and Edie, and his son, Frank A., along with six grandchildren lived close by. They took turns bringing him food in the evenings.

It was Edie's turn to bring him dinner on that cold February night. About 5:45 p.m., she and her husband, David, came to the house with a hot meal and some clean clothing. She opened the front door as usual and walked in but was horror-struck by what she saw. Her father was lying on the floor. The eighty-six-year-old had been beaten, bound and gagged. Edie dropped the laundry she was carrying, and she and David ran to the neighbors to call the police.

Richmond Heights Police sergeant Edward "Tom" Zelazny and patrolmen Joseph T. Steffen and William Meyers responded to the call and were followed by Detective Robert Zelina and Patrolman Jim Gentille. While Meyers, Zelina and Gentille entered the house from the back door, Zelazny and Steffin went in the front.

Zelazny wrote in his report that they found Frank in the living room with his hands and feet bound with the telephone cord. His face was covered with what looked to him at first like a brown rag. Zelazny lifted the rag and found that a piece of it was wrapped around Frank's mouth and neck as a gag. The brown "rag" was later identified as one of Frank's shirts. It looked as though the grandfather of six had been struck on the forehead with a blunt instrument, and he had not survived the attack.

Frank Noch came to the United States from Germany as a young man of nineteen and settled in the Cleveland area. *Courtesy of Edie Metz.*

Meyers, Zelina and Gentille found that entry to the house had been made through the back door, which was not visible from the street. The storm door was unlocked, and the screen was torn. The wooden exterior door was standing open and its lower glass pane smashed. A snow shovel had been used as a prop between the two doors.

As Meyer and Zelina searched the attached garage and the basement, Steffin and Zelazny checked the sitting room, kitchen, back bedroom, bath and three bedrooms upstairs. No one else was in the house.

Frank was not a big man at 5'9" and 165 pounds, but he was strong, his grandson Mark said. "He had phenomenal strength." To illustrate, he recounted the story of his grandfather carrying a baby grand piano on his back up three flights of stairs to an apartment, and the only help he needed was a man on each side to keep the instrument balanced. Because

Frank Noch built a greenhouse and grew many plants from white and purple orchids to cacti. *Cleveland Public Library Photo Collection.*

of Frank's excellent physical condition, the family felt it was likely it took more than one intruder to subdue him.

A few days later, the coroner ruled that Frank had died of a "crushing impact to the trunk with multiple rib fractures and asphyxia."

Although it was not noted in the initial police incident report, family members later learned that several Italian cigarette butts were found on the ground by the back door. Frank did not smoke. Could those cigarette butts have belonged to a lookout who was waiting while his or her accomplice(s) were in the house beating the elderly man and hunting for items to steal?

Edie told police that a TV, a watch, some money and jewelry were missing. Nothing of true value was stolen, but the thugs had broken the lock on a desk that her father had handcrafted and definitely rifled through it. She said her father did not have much money or many items of value in the house. He lived on his pensions from General Motors and the German army.

The case was turned over to Richmond Heights police detective Michael LoPresti. He and Steffin started the investigation by canvasing the neighborhood but learned nothing. LoPresti told the *Plain Dealer* that Frank was found wearing slippers. That led the detective to believe Frank was at home when he was attacked instead of coming home and surprising the intruders. LoPresti said Frank was hard of hearing and was not wearing his hearing aid. That made it possible he did not hear them break the glass panel in the back door to get in the house.

Funeral services were held on Thursday, February 23, at 1:00 p.m. at the Brickman & Sons Funeral Home. He was buried at Acacia Masonic

Memorial Park Cemetery in Mayfield Heights next to his wife, Marie, who died in 1973.

Frank Noch was born in Essen, Germany, on November 16, 1897, to Julius and Mary (Pulsz) Noch. He was a member of the German army and fought in World War I. During the war, he was wounded in the leg. After recovering, he came to the United States at the age of nineteen. As he was leaving Germany, his father told him he would be back. When he did go back to Germany, it was only to visit his family. He never went back to stay. Instead, he became a U.S. citizen in 1925.

A friend sponsored him to come to Cleveland, where he met and fell in love with Marie Wilhelmine Kull, who was also from Germany. They were married in March 1929.

Frank worked for the Fisher Body Division of General Motors in Cleveland. As a machinist and tool and die maker there, he designed an advanced measuring tool that made him a valued employee to the plant.

Frank kept busy with friends after retiring in 1963. He enjoyed playing skat, a German card game similar to bridge, and performed with a German singing group. His fenced-in backyard on Beverly Hills Drive was large, where he kept two chickens and a duck. At one time, he had a rooster named Hans and a German shepherd. Frank built a small greenhouse in the yard. "He raised amazing things," Mark said, "orchids and coffee bean plants." He also raised different kinds of cactus.

Mark said his grandfather spent a lot of time with him and his two brothers. "He had lots of tools. He built a sawmill, a chicken coop, and he made furniture. He'd teach us how to make these projects. He even taught us plumbing."

After two weeks under the tutelage from his wife's nephew, Frank was making mobiles of eye-catching fish out of different colors of paper ribbon and sparklers for eyes. Next, he made wooden boat mobiles. He used black walnut, rosewood, mahogany and lacewood and worked with the shavings to make the ships' sails. He donated many of his mobiles to hospitals and sold others.

As a young man, he enjoyed woodworking. Once he was retired, he went back to the craft and made furniture, including the desk that the thugs broke into and ransacked.

Six days after the murder, Crime Stoppers of Cuyahoga County stepped in to offer a $2,000 reward for information leading to an arrest and indictment. Crime Stoppers describes its function thus: "Encourages members of the community to assist local law enforcement agencies in the fight against crime

Right: Frank Noch made wooden mobiles in the shape of ships. *Courtesy of Edie Metz.*

Below: Frank Noch donated many of his mobiles to hospitals, and others were sold at the Sassy Cat in Chagrin Falls. *Cleveland Public Library Photo Collection.*

by overcoming the two key elements that inhibit community involvement: fear and apathy." Tipsters who call the hotline at 216-252-7463 can remain anonymous. Frank Noch's family pledged $5,000 to the reward a few months later. Former Richmond Heights mayor H. Donald Zimmerman also started a reward fund at National City Bank. After so many years, these rewards may no longer be offered.

In a 2022 interview for an article on Cleveland.com ("After 38 Years Richmond Heights Police Have Teamed with Ohio BCI to Try to Find Frank Noch's Killers"), LoPresti told Jeff Piorkowski that the intruders were in the house long enough to search through all the rooms. He said they took Frank's wallet out of his pocket, possibly leaving touch DNA on his pants that could be used to confirm a match.

LoPresti retired from the Richmond Heights Police Department in 1999 and went to work at the Bureau of Criminal Investigation (BCI). He told Cleveland.com that the detective bureau at the time of Frank's death was "thin and not experienced in handling such cases." He reached out to other cities for help from experienced detectives. But in the end, there was not enough evidence to identify and arrest any suspects.

The only witness was a UPS driver, who told LoPresti he saw a late-model dark brown Ford LTD station wagon in Frank's driveway, but the driver's memory was hazy. "He didn't remember much, but we had him put under hypnosis, and he remembered a lot." LoPresti told Piorkowski, "We tried anything we could." LoPresti said the UPS driver was not sure how many people were in the car. In addition, the car's windows were tinted, so he could not give a description of anyone in the car. LoPresti did not elaborate on anything more the UPS driver may have recalled.

Richmond Heights Community Park at 27285 Highland Road behind Richmond Heights City Hall was dedicated to Frank Noch a year later.

Today, Frank's daughter Edie Metz enjoys having some of her father's handmade furniture—such as a black walnut end table—in her house. Frank's handmade desk that the killers broke into is also in her home, but she keeps it in a spot where she does not see it. "It's upstairs. I just can't look at it because that's what they broke into," she said softly. She said at one time she thought she might have it destroyed, but decided against it because her dad made the piece.

Anyone with information about the murder of Frank Noch can submit a tip to the Richmond Heights Police Department (216-486-1234) or Crime Stoppers.

4

CAMPUS COED STILL MISSING AFTER FOUR DECADES

Judy Martins was just twenty-two years old when she vanished off the campus of Kent State University in the wee hours of May 24, 1978. She had been at a party at Dunbar Hall, a boy's dormitory, the evening before. Witnesses claim she left the party on Wednesday at 2:30 a.m. when the party began to wind down and only a few people were left. She supposedly disappeared while going back to Engleman Hall, where she lived. The pathway has changed after all these years, but the walk took her behind Prentice Hall and past some large bushes—no more than a five-minute walk. She never made it and has never been seen again.

More than four decades later, Judy's younger sister, Nancy Baer, still thinks of her and misses her every day. "We were really, really close," Nancy said. "She was so much fun. My girlfriends all wanted a sister like her."

"She was a great older sister," Judy and Nancy's younger brother, Steve Martins, said.

Born on July 15, 1955, to Dolores, a nurse, and Arthur, an Avon Lake employee, Judy was the oldest of three. The Martins had lived in Avon Lake since before their three children were born.

Judy graduated from Avon Lake High School in 1973 and had lots of friends. "She was a class officer (senior-year secretary) and on the honor roll," Nancy said. "She was smart and artsy."

Her brother, Steve, agreed. "She was very, very intelligent. She was a deep thinker. I had some of her textbooks, and in reading the notations she wrote in the side of pages, I saw how she thought."

Judy Martins was a resident student advisor in Engleman Hall where she lived on campus. *U.S. Marshals Service, Cleveland Office.*

Judy started college at Ohio University, but after two years she was not sure what she wanted to major in. She came home to Avon Lake to figure it out. A year and a half later, she enrolled at Kent State University as a junior. At first, she took general courses. She took English, and Steve said she was an excellent writer. She also became interested in women's studies and was thinking she might like to become a therapist or counselor. At the time she went missing, she was a resident advisor (RA) in her dormitory and was a volunteer counselor for female Kent State students.

Steve remembered how Judy always saw the best in people and gave them the benefit of the doubt. He and Nancy had better radar when it came to sizing people up, he said, adding, "Judy was very compassionate and was always trying to help people."

Nancy, who had moved to Columbus before Judy's disappearance, vividly remembers driving home to Avon Lake in a torrential downpour on Tuesday night, May 23, 1978, to pick up a new car. It was the end of spring quarter, so Judy was expected to come home the next day to pick up Nancy's car. The storm worried Dolores that night. "Mom was relieved when I got there. She was afraid something bad would happen." The girls' mother may have had a premonition, Nancy said.

But Judy did not show up to pick up her car on Wednesday or Thursday, and she did not call. It was unlike her to not check in with her family.

Judy did not have a roommate, so no one in Engleman Hall realized she was gone until that Friday (May 26), and then they started to call her home.

"Mom had three phone calls Friday asking if Judy was home," Nancy said. "Apparently they thought she came home for the Memorial Day weekend." Dolores became frantic after that and started calling Judy's dorm room every hour. She got no answer. There was talk of Judy going to New York with friends for the holiday weekend. If that was true, those friends may have been the ones who called her home in Avon Lake.

Another RA student reported her missing.

Theories and sightings began to circulate. The theories were all out of character for Nancy and Steve's sister. Three people saw a young woman resembling Judy at a garage sale who spoke of hitchhiking to Mexico and working as a waitress. A Kent man told campus police that he had picked up a hitchhiker who looked like Judy. He let her off in Barberton. It turned out that neither of these women was Judy Martins.

When her room was searched, all of her belongings—glasses, makeup, clothing, money, student ID and her one credit card—were still there, untouched.

Steve told a *Beacon Journal* staff writer that she wore contacts and would never leave her glasses behind. Nancy told the same reporter that she rarely went anywhere without her makeup. Both Steve and Nancy agreed that Judy would never have left of her own accord. She was happy at Kent. She had friends and was involved in campus life. And she was responsible.

It took a few days before the police began to look for Judy in earnest. According to a 2013 *Record Courier* article by Dave O'Brien, KSU and Kent police searched the city, the Standing Rock area and the Cuyahoga River banks and even borrowed a National Guard helicopter with infrared scanners—all to no avail. John Peach, detective for the Kent city police at the time and who later became KSU's police chief, told the newspaper that police did not find any evidence of foul play. However, Peach did tell O'Brien that Judy's disappearance was a "real mystery."

Some people, including Judy's boyfriend of five years with whom she had recently broken up, were given lie detectors and were eliminated. Police never had any solid suspects. The only person of interest in Judy's disappearance was a man named William John Posey Jr., according to the Charley Project website, which maintains a database of missing persons. He apparently lived within ten minutes from the campus under an assumed name. He had abducted and killed an Illinois woman two years earlier and was a suspect in the death of a woman in 1980. He wound up in prison in North Carolina.

Coed Judy Martins was twenty-two years old when she went missing off the Kent State University campus in 1978. *Courtesy of Nancy Martins Baer.*

Judy Martins wore a curly red wig as a joke to a party at Dunbar Hall. *U.S. Marshals Service, Cleveland Office.*

A few weeks after Judy's disappearance, the Martins family met with then KSU president Brage Golding. They came away from the meeting disappointed, with the feeling that Golding just wanted the situation to go away. It was eight years after the May 4, 1970 shooting, and the administration did not want to draw any more negative attention to the university.

Two years after Judy vanished, the Cuyahoga County jail had a woman in custody who bore a resemblance to Judy. Booked on a prostitution charge, the drug-addicted woman gave her name as Judy Martinez and her birth date the same as Judy's. Dolores hoped it was her daughter, but Arthur went to see the woman and said she was definitely not their Judy.

Someone else saw a prostitute in the bars on Prospect Avenue in Cleveland and said she looked like Judy. "My mom was desperate to find anything out," Steve said, so he went to Cleveland and was able to locate the prostitute. Although she looked similar to his sister, he was able to rule her out.

The police disposed of the Judy Martins file in 2000, claiming the department's retention policy. Peach told a *Record Courier* writer that "it was never classified a crime." He said it happened before any guidelines were established to confirm an individual was indeed missing, and there was no DNA testing and no electronic records at the time. The 1978 Kent city police chief, Ron Heineking, said disappearances at that time were not publicized much.

The last time Nancy saw her sister was on her twenty-first birthday, a few weeks before Judy vanished. Judy gave Nancy a card that read, "To a very special sister…with very special thoughts of all we've shared." The message was fitting for two young women who were so close. Judy added that Nancy's present would be a subscription to whatever magazine she chose. Nancy has saved that card all these years.

Above: Before Judy Martins disappeared, she sent her sister, Nancy, this twenty-first birthday card. *Courtesy of Nancy Martins Baer.*

Right: A fitting birthday message for sisters who were so close. *Courtesy of Nancy Martins Baer.*

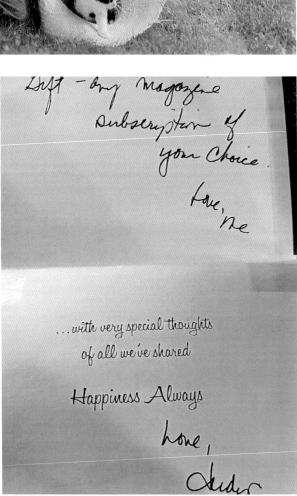

Judy's parents died never knowing what happened to their oldest child. Arthur was never the same after Judy went missing. He passed away of cancer in 1990 at only fifty-seven. Nancy believes Judy's disappearance contributed to his death. Dolores never gave up hope that her daughter would be found and regularly called police for updates. She was seventy-one when she died in 2003 "of a broken heart."

The U.S. marshal for the Northern District of Ohio, Pete Elliott, got involved in Judy's case around 2020. He sent deputy marshals to track down and interview those KSU students (now scattered all over the United States) who were at that party or in the area of the campus at the time. Elliot said he is confident he will find out what happened. He interviewed William Posey at the federal prison in Butner, North Carolina, three times and is certain that Posey had nothing to do with Judy's disappearance.

"They [the marshals] have been wonderful," Nancy said, adding that Marshal Elliott has kept them up to date.

Judy Martins was a beautiful young woman with long dark brown hair and brown eyes. She was 5'4" tall and weighed 120 pounds. She had a small scar on the left side of her forehead, and she had pierced ears. At the time she went missing, she was wearing a yellow and brown gauze blouse, midcalf blue jean culottes with a brown belt, a trench coat and brown boots. She

Judy Martins (*center*) with her brother, Steve, and sister, Nancy. *Courtesy of Nancy Martins Baer.*

carried a big white imitation leather bag. She was wearing a curly red wig as a joke.

If she left that party and was accosted on the short pathway to her dorm, it seems as though she would have screamed and fought. Prentice Hall was in the area. Although it was 2:30 in the morning, it was the end of spring break and near the Memorial Day holiday, so it is possible other students were outside. Surely someone would have heard or seen something.

If anyone has any information, they should call U.S. Marshal Pete Elliott at 216-522-4482.

"It has hung over my life every day. There's never any closure," Nancy said.

"We're not looking for retribution," Steve said. "We're just looking for closure."

5

BRISTOLVILLE PARENTS OF FIVE DISAPPEAR

F riday, December 15, 1995, was Johnny Markley's eighth birthday. His mom, Shelly, put him on the school bus at 8:30 a.m. His four older sisters, Ruth, Stacey, Bonnie and Chrystal, were all already off to school. Their dad, John, was home that morning because his twin sister, Bonnie Donaldson, had died two days earlier after a three-year battle with breast cancer. Other than that, it was a normal day for the five kids. Until…

That afternoon, when the five Markley kids came home from school, they found Shelly, thirty-two, and John, thirty-six, were not at home. Their parents' 1990 red and gray Chevy pickup was gone, and the door to the house was unlocked.

The children looked around the house. Shelly's purse, along with her wallet, was in the kitchen. Her Marlboro cigarettes, cigarette case and a lighter were lying next to a half cup of coffee. Shelly smoked a pack a day, so it was unusual for her to go out without her cigarettes. The coffee pot was still on the stove and nearly boiled dry. John's wristwatch was sitting on the shelf by the stove. That also struck the Markley children as odd because he never went anywhere without it. He always put it on first thing in the morning.

Upstairs, the children found the gun cabinet in their parents' bedroom standing open. Without fail, John kept the cabinet locked so the children could not access the guns. A small safe (or lock box) John and Shelly kept in their closet was sitting open on the bathroom sink, and birth certificates and other papers were scattered around the room.

The clothing Shelly and John had planned to wear to Bonnie's calling hours that evening was laid out on the unmade bed.

John and Shelly were devoted parents, and it was highly unlikely that they would leave their children unattended without even a note indicating where they had gone.

John's sister Judy Yeager and her husband, Tom, lived a few miles down Route 88 and often watched the children when the Markleys went out. The children called them and went to their house that day to wait for their parents to come home. At first, Judy was sure it was just a miscommunication and her brother and sister-in-law would be home soon. But they did not come home.

The calling hours at the funeral home for Bonnie started at 5:30 p.m. Judy and Tom took the children to the funeral home, convinced that John and Shelly would turn up there. But the calling hours came and went, and John and Shelly did not show up.

Judy became increasingly worried. She and her husband called the area hospitals and taxi companies. Then they called the airlines and bus terminals. Finally, at 12:30 a.m., they called the Trumbull County Sheriff's Department and reported John and Shelly missing.

Detectives responded to the Markleys and looked around the house but found no forced entry. The children told deputies they didn't know how many firearms their father owned, so they had no idea if any were missing from the gun cabinet. Deputies checked the guns, but none had been fired recently. Two tarps John used to cover his 1978 red Corvette in the garage were missing. John's siblings told police this was concerning because he always kept the car covered. One thing they did not find in the house was the couple's checkbook.

In talking to the family, detectives learned that John had been distraught over his twin sister's death. He had prayed for her recovery and even gone so far as to raise $15,000 for her to have an experimental treatment in Mexico. Her death had made him bitter and caused him to lose his faith in God.

The family had faced other tragedies in the two years before Bonnie's death. Their house burned down in 1993. The next year, John's father passed away. A few months after that, a nephew died by suicide.

Police wondered if it all was too much for John, so the two simply disappeared.

But still, it was unthinkable that John and Shelly would just up and leave. The couple married in November 1979 when Shelly was only sixteen and John was twenty. They had been married for sixteen years. Their four daughters were all born a year apart. Then four years later their son came along.

Born in Valdosta, Georgia, John was one of ten children. He had no criminal record. He was an independent long-distance truck driver. He provided well for the family. Their rural four-bedroom, two-a-half-bath house on Route 88 (Greenville Road) in Bristolville was paid off. He had no life insurance.

Originally from Warren, Shelly Renee Applequist went to Warren G. Harding High School. She had two brothers and two sisters. She was a stay-at-home mom who dearly loved and cared for her children. Their freezer was fully stocked with food for the winter. They had recently taken out a $1,500 loan for new tires on John's semi and deposited it in their checking account. It just made no sense that they would leave of their own choosing.

The family held out hope that John and Shelly would be back for the funeral and went about cleaning and readying the house in preparation for guests the next day, Saturday.

Their hope was dashed on Saturday afternoon when John and Shelly's 1990 Chevy pickup was located by family members. It had been abandoned ten miles from their home on Elm Road in the Stambaugh Hardware store parking lot near the Perkins Restaurant in Howland.

At that, investigators' thoughts turned to foul play. For one thing, the truck was covered in mud as if it had been taken off-road. One newspaper account said someone had written "wash me" in the dirt. John never took the pickup off-road, instead keeping it in immaculate condition. Sheriff Thomas Altiere told the *Vindicator*, "On Monday somebody saying they were Markley called the Stambaugh Thompson store on Elm Road asking for information on who towed their truck." He added, "We don't know right now if the call was bogus or not."

The truck was locked, and the keys were missing. The couple's phone was in the truck. Strangely, the two tarps that had covered John's Corvette were in the bed of the truck along with a semi-size tire. Detectives verified that the vehicle had no mechanical problems and was drivable.

Authorities called out helicopters to search Bristolville, Champion, Farmington and Howland from the air. Neighbors and friends joined the search on the ground in the area of the couple's home.

Searchers dragged the swamp in the Grand River Wildlife area not far from the Markleys' home. Nelson Ledges, Lake Milton and Mosquito Lake were all searched by divers. Cadaver dogs were brought in. No evidence of John and Shelly turned up in any of the searches.

Investigators checked for transactions on their bank account at the Cortland Bank in North Bloomfield and learned that at 10:36 a.m. on the day John and Shelly disappeared, they cashed a personal check for $1,000 at the drive-up window. The teller was familiar with the Markleys and recognized them. She remembered there were three people in the truck. John was driving, and Shelly was sitting in the middle of her husband and a third man. The teller could not get a good look at the other man, but she told detectives he was slender and had dark hair. Shelly made out the check to cash while they were in the truck, the teller said. The transaction was peculiar, because they were withdrawing the funds that they had borrowed for a set of semi-truck tires. The withdrawal left a balance of $865 in their account.

Christmas came and went. The aunts and uncles did what they could for the children. One of the uncles brought in a tree, and the family decorated it. John's sister Linda Mason told the papers, "Over Christmas and New Years, we kept telling the kids their mom and dad will be home soon." Young Johnny wrote a note to Santa that said all he wanted for Christmas was his mom and dad.

Linda and her husband, Gene, were from Salisbury, North Carolina, but they stayed on after the holidays at John and Shelly's house so the children could remain in the familiar setting of their own home.

On New Year's Eve at 1:30 p.m., a man with a raspy voice called the Markley home and talked with Linda Mason. He claimed to be holding John and Shelly for ransom and said he would release them in exchange for $10,000 cash. He gave them until 5:00 p.m. Linda immediately called the sheriff's office.

The story was recounted in the *Cleveland Plain Dealer* on February 23, 1997. The next events resembled a scene straight out of a movie.

By the time the raspy-voiced man called back, sheriff's detective Wayne Cardarelli had given the Masons a device that suctioned to the phone so the call could be recorded. This time, Gene answered the phone when it rang. The voice on the other end told him to go to a telephone booth at the Rally's restaurant near the Eastwood Mall in Warren. There, Mason would find a note in the return change slot with instructions on how to deliver the money. It was Sunday, and there was most likely no way to gather $10,000 in cash, so Mason and the detective stuffed dish towels instead of money into a bag. Cardarelli then followed Mason in a separate car to the telephone booth. The detective went to the booth and found a lengthy note scrawled in a childish hand with many misspellings. The note said to go to the mall and park in front of the Kaufman's entrance and go into the store, where he was to find the sweatshirts with a "penguin bird" (Youngstown State's mascot Pete the Penguin) on them. The note said to place the package (money, which was really dish towels) in among the shirts and then leave the store by the same door he had entered. Next, he was to drive to the JCPenny's entrance and go in, where there was a telephone next to the restrooms, and wait for fifteen minutes. The note warned that if things did not "look right" or any law was around, the deal was off. If things looked clear, a boy would hand him a note with an address on it.

While Mason followed the instructions on the note, Detective Michael Davis was posing as a shopper and keeping an eye on the bag of dish towels. Although a man, a woman and a boy stopped to look at the sweatshirts, they did not appear to pay any attention to the bag.

After a while, Gene Mason and Detective Cardarelli reconnoitered in the parking lot and decided to try again in case the raspy-voiced man had been delayed for some reason. That was not going to work, because the man had called Markleys' home and told Linda Mason, "I see the cops. You people are not following directions."

Even though the caller knew law enforcement was involved, he did not call it off. Instead, he issued a new set of directions. This time, Mason was to go to a Sunoco station/convenience store a half mile away and leave the bag in the restroom wastebasket. Mason did as he was told.

Cardarelli and other deputies were watching from a strip mall across the street when someone in a hooded jacket appeared and entered the restroom. A white car pulled around to the door as the person came out of the restroom. A man was driving the car. When the hooded figure climbed into the car, the waiting deputies moved in.

The driver of the car was forty-five-year-old Stephen (spelled Steven in some accounts) Durst of Warren. The person in the hooded jacket was a pregnant nineteen-year-old Deanna Durst, Stephen's daughter. Detective Davis recognized Durst as the man in Kaufman's who was looking at the sweatshirts with two other people. Durst was arrested and charged with extortion. His daughter was not charged.

Investigators learned that Durst had been friends with Markley at one time. Durst had been out of a job, was cash-strapped and needed a place to stay with his two children. Markley not only gave Durst a job driving a second semi but also allowed him and his children to stay in his home with his family. According to the same *Cleveland Plain Dealer* article, things changed when Markley fired Durst over a money dispute in the summer of 1995. He kicked Durst's family out of his home and withheld his paycheck. Durst told people that Markley owed him $1,000—the same amount as the check the Markeys cashed the morning they went missing.

While some thought Durst was just an opportunist, others thought he was involved in the Markleys' disappearance in some way. Jane Timko, who took over the investigation in 1996, said, "I truly believe that Steven Durst knows what happened to them and he just won't say."

Durst volunteered to take a lie detector test. The results indicated that he was not being truthful when asked if he had anything to do with or knew anything about the Markleys' disappearance. In August, he was convicted of extortion, and Trumbull County common pleas judge Andrew D. Logan sentenced him to a four-to-ten-year term at the Marion Correctional Facility. Durst appealed the conviction, but it was turned down.

Trumbull County sheriff Thomas Altiere said his investigators spent eleven months and tracked down hundreds of leads that went nowhere. In December 1996, he told the press, "My gut instinct is that they died. No solid evidence, but if they were still alive, they would have left some type of trail like credit card receipts."

The disappearance of the Markleys has been aired on *Unsolved Mysteries*. The family appeared on *The Montel Williams Show*, where psychic Silvia Browne told them John and Shelly were in the water near Bowling Green. They also told the story on the *Maury* show.

In December 2015, Sheriff Altiere announced that they had new information. He told Channel 21 WFMS that they had gotten new leads right around the twentieth anniversary of the Markeys' disappearance. The leads came in the form of interviews, he said. "We just need that one tidbit to come up with and we can hopefully do some indictments."

Those leads evidently did not pan out.

On April 9, 2020, Trumbull sheriff's deputies were called to a house on High Oakfield Road W, five miles and a seven-minute drive from where the Markleys lived. Deputies found that seventy-one-year-old Milton Kurtzman had shot his roommate, Allen Byler, sixty-four, multiple times in the abdomen. According to a WKBN report, deputies had responded to a call at that same address in February. At that time, Byler told authorities Kurtzman was beginning to show signs of dementia, and having loaded firearms around the house made him uneasy.

Kurtzman was taken into custody along with a .357 Sig Sauer. He died in his jail cell the next night. The coroner called it natural causes.

After the shooting, the sheriff's department began to take a deeper look into the property. The television station reported that authorities learned some information while investigating the shooting that led them to believe there may have been additional crimes committed on the fifty acres of property.

Several deputies, the Bureau of Criminal Investigation and the FBI, as well as an excavator, were called in to help with the search. Searchers looked through vehicles and buildings.

Trumbull County sheriff Paul Monroe told WKBN that law enforcement learned the crime scene they were first called to went beyond the house. Acting on information that more crimes had been committed on the property, law enforcement hunted to recover any evidence.

Although Monroe would not say what the crime(s) or evidence was, he did say that any clues found could help solve a crime that dated back twenty years.

Thoughts went to the disappearance of the Markleys.

What was found—if anything—was never revealed, and so the Markleys remain missing.

6

GOLD COAST EXECUTIVE SLAIN

By 9:30 on Thursday morning October 16, 1980, Norm Liver (pronounced with a long *i*, as in *alive*) had not shown up for work. That was not like the fifty-seven-year-old bachelor, who was the executive vice president and operating officer of the Lee Turzillo Contracting Company in Richfield.

Without exception, he would tell the company's receptionist, Ellen Lane, or his secretary, Mary Kraus, if he was going to be later than his normal 8:30 a.m. arrival, and if he was going to be late, he would let one of them know where he would be. But there was no call from him that morning, and Ellen remembered that he had not mentioned anything when he left work at 5:00 p.m. on Wednesday.

Part of Ellen's job was to make travel arrangements, including airline reservations, for the corporate employees traveling for business, so she knew he was not out of town. She vividly remembered the feeling that something was not right.

She tried calling his home on the Gold Coast of Lakewood periodically throughout the morning, but the phone rang and rang. She looked up the number for his close friend Patty (last name forgotten with time), who worked for United Airlines, but got no answer there. Ellen was used to making appointments for him, so she tried his dentist office, but he was not on the books for that morning.

By this time, Lucille Turzillo (my mother), widow of company founder Lee Turzillo (my father), had come in to work. After my father's death in July

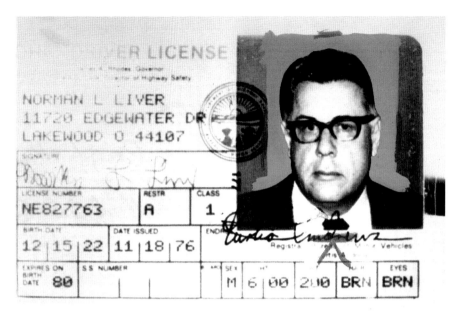

Norman L. Liver's Ohio driver's license. *Cleveland State University, Michael Schwartz Library, Special Collections.*

1977, she took over the company as president. She did not have the business acumen or the vast knowledge of concrete and foundations that my father had. He was one of the foremost authorities on foundation construction and placement and concrete repairs at the time. Although my mother sat at his desk in his office, the actual company's operations rested on Norm's shoulders, so she became upset when Ellen could not get hold of him.

Approaching lunchtime, Ellen's immediate boss, John Monde, the firm's secretary, suggested she call the building management at the Lake Erie waterside Edgewater Towers high-rise apartment building on Edgewater Drive where Norm lived. On that call, Ellen asked desk clerk Benjamin L. Cohn to check the garage to see if Norm's Oldsmobile Toronado was there. He called back a few minutes later and confirmed the car was in its usual parking space.

A few minutes later, Ellen and John decided it was time to call back and ask Cohn to check Norm's apartment. Cohn said he would call back. When enough time went by with no call back, Ellen became impatient and dialed Cohn again.

Ellen remembered the total shock in Cohn's voice when he answered her call. He had found Norm dead at 12:30 p.m. when he unlocked the door to the first-floor luxury two-bedroom apartment where he had lived since 1957. Cohn alerted the building superintendent, William Mumaw. Mumaw's wife, June, went to the apartment.

Deluxe high-rise apartment buildings on Lakewood's Gold Coast. Edgewater Towers is the first building on the left. *Cleveland Public Library Photo Collection.*

According to *Cleveland Press* reporter Wally Guenther, June Mumaw said, "He (Liver) was nude and half of his body was in the closet with the legs in the hallway."

Lying face up near his bedroom, he had suffered several stab wounds to the neck and trunk. His genitals had been cut off after death and taken. His clothing was in a heap on the floor in the living room.

Although our family and the company employees had known Norm for many years—he had been present for weddings, christenings, funerals and the company's annual ox roast—there was one thing we did not know about him.

John Monde told the press that Norm was personable. He cared about the people he worked with, yet he was somewhat aloof. The building's superintendent called him a good tenant who paid his $320 monthly rent on time. He said the building's residents liked Norm and he did not seem to have any enemies. June Mumaw told the *Cleveland Press* that Norm was "a quiet, neat, clean and well-mannered man."

The night before his death, he and a neighbor went out for ice cream. He was last seen in the laundry room around 9:00 p.m. A resident across the hall told the paper he heard some loud "thumps" coming from Norm's apartment around 10:00 p.m. but did not think much about it, as Norm gave frequent parties. Other residents said that he had many male visitors. Those of us who knew him had no idea of his life outside the office.

According to the *Plain Dealer*, Lakewood's police captain William L. Stevens led the investigation and could find no immediate motive or suspect. Police found no evidence of forced entry, leading them to believe Norm knew his assailant. Lieutenant Ronald Hall told the *Cleveland Press* that Norm's attacker "was more than a casual acquaintance who apparently was very angry at him."

Police did not believe anything of value had been stolen. They collected knives from the kitchen and turned them over to the coroner to check for blood residue, but no murder weapon was recovered at the time. Lakewood detectives sifted through the building's incinerator looking for clues but found nothing to help them.

Stevens said police needed to talk with "several suspects, including one woman." Detectives questioned neighbors, associates and employees of the Turzillo company; they dismissed all of them as suspects. Cleveland Metro Parks divers searched Lake Erie behind the apartment complex in hopes of finding any leads, particularly the murder weapon, but they came up empty-handed.

The coroner discovered bruises, abrasions and scratches on Norm's face, neck and left elbow, and he had sustained cuts on his palms, fingers

The tree-lined residential area of Lakewood where Norman Liver lived. *Cleveland Public Library Photo Collection.*

and right forearm. All of this suggested he struggled with his attacker. The cause of death was listed as multiple stab wounds, including penetration to the left lung.

When no arrests had been made by December 1980, the Northern Ohio Coalition Inc. (an organization composed of business leaders in the GLBT community of Northern Ohio) offered a $1,000 reward for information about the murders of Norman Liver and Lee Wrightnour of Rocky River. Wrightnour's murder was cleared with the arrest of brothers Mark K. and James M. Spear. No connection to Norm's death was reported in the papers, and the murder methods were different.

In January 1981, police turned to Burton Leidner, a certified member of the Society of Investigative and Forensic Hypnosis at the time. He had worked for the FBI's Cleveland office and the Ohio State Highway Patrol, as well as area police departments, and had been called in on seventy-nine cases the previous year. He hypnotized two residents from Edgewater Towers where Norm lived, but there was no report on what, if anything, was learned.

Born in Gallion, Alabama, on December 15, 1922, the only child of Norman Lary Liver Sr. and Elizabeth Collins Liver, he grew up on the family-owned farm. He developed an interest in engineering from his uncle who worked for the Army Corps of Engineers. After graduating from the Polytechnic Institute (Auburn University) with a degree in engineering, he received his master's degree in soil mechanics from the University of Illinois.

He and my father worked together at Intrusion-Prepakt Inc. of Cleveland for twenty years. When my father left that company to form the Lee Turzillo Contracting Company in 1955, Norm went with him.

Norm was a nationally known and highly respected expert on foundation work and was often sought as a consultant. In addition, he frequently served as an expert witness in civil lawsuits.

Plain Dealer reporters contacted Norm's mother, Elizabeth, who was eighty-six years old at the time of her son's death. She described him as a devoted son who called her several times a week and regularly visited her on the farm in Demopolis, Alabama. His father died in 1952. His mother died in 1995 at the age of one hundred.

Norm is buried alongside his parents in the Saint Andrews Episcopal Cemetery in Prairieville, Alabama.

7

DNA IDENTIFIES SANDUSKY'S JANE DOE

On Sunday March 30, 1980, two Sandusky residents were on their regular early morning walk along the Lake Erie coastline. At the 1200 block of the Cedar Point causeway, they saw some wood debris washed up on the beach. A closer look revealed the badly decomposed body of a woman caught up on a log.

The fire department pulled the body out of the water, and the Sandusky police started what would become a four-decade-long investigation. The deputy Erie County coroner, Carl Winans, pronounced the woman dead at 8:30 a.m. at the water's edge and ordered her body to be taken to the Frey-Goff Funeral Home for further examination. She had been in the water for some time and was so badly decomposed that she could not be identified. All Winans could tell was that she was Caucasian, of average height, with an average to slender build. Beyond that, there was nothing on her to tell who she was or where she was from. Her hair was gone. Her face was distorted from the water. She had no scars. She was wearing a faded brown or tan size 12 dress from Sears, a white lace petticoat, a white bra, blue and green flowered panties and shredded pantyhose. Her ears were pierced, but she was not wearing earrings or any other jewelry. She had no shoes.

The Erie County Coroner's Office was not able to handle a case like this at the time, so she was sent to the Cuyahoga County Medical Examiner in Cleveland for an autopsy, which was performed the next day.

Cuyahoga County coroner Ross E. Zumwalt determined she died from blunt force impact to her trunk with multiple rib fractures, lacerations of the liver and kidney and fractures of the pelvis. He found lacerations on her scalp and various contusions on her body. Her left arm was fractured in two places. The autopsy did not report any stab wounds or bullet holes. Her manner of death could not be determined. The traumas could have been caused by the lake ice, wave action against the rocks or a fall from a high place. The coroner could not tell whether the injuries occurred before or after death. The icy conditions of the water could have preserved her body for a period of time, possibly delaying decomposition. Dr. Zumwalt's best guess on her time of death was the late summer or fall of 1979.

She was estimated to be in her late twenties or early thirties. She was 5'5½"–5'6" tall and weighed 130 pounds. Several teeth were missing, and others were decayed.

Cuyahoga County returned her to the Frey-Goff Funeral Home in Sandusky, and they buried her at Sand Hill Cemetery, Section B, Lot 65, Grave 3, as Jane Doe.

Sandusky police did not think she was local. Detective W. Weber began sending teletypes to numerous Northern Ohio police agencies, requesting any information on missing white women. They began to receive leads.

One of the most interesting was from Mrs. Arthur Martins of Avon Lake. She was looking for her daughter Judy Martins, who had gone missing in 1978 from the Kent State University campus one evening after a party. Her daughter was twenty-two years old, 5'4" tall and weighed 120 pounds. The coed wore a dress size 8 or 9. Mrs. Martins said her daughter had good teeth with only one cavity. The general description did not match.

Bentley, West Virginia police reached out with the hope that Sandusky's Jane Doe was Juanita Reidy. She disappeared after leaving her husband and withdrawing $5,000 from their joint savings account. She and the money left with another man. Police located her burned-out car, but Juanita was missing. Her husband got hold of her dental records from her dentist and sent them to Sandusky, but there was no match.

There was no progress for the next several years, and the case went cold. Then in 2020, the U.S. Marshals Service revived the investigation after finding a 1980 teletype in a file the Avon Police Department had for the disappearance of Judy Martins. She was the Avon resident and Kent State University student who had vanished from campus in 1978. Northern District of Ohio U.S. Marshal Pete Elliott wrote to Erie County sheriff Paul A. Sigsworth asking to have Jane Doe exhumed. Elliott said he knew she did not match Judy Martins physically, but she could help with other missing women. Elliott wrote, "We believe that by exhuming DNA from the

The Cedar Point Causeway in Sandusky along Lake Erie's beautiful coastline. *Photo by Tom Horsman, City Manager's Office, the City of Sandusky.*

Sandusky Jane Doe that there would be a great probability of it matching a missing person case currently outstanding."

In late fall of 2020, Deputy U.S. Marshal Bill Boldin and Sandusky's detective Gary Wichman worked with the Lucus County Coroner's Office to have Jane Doe exhumed.

Nine samples were collected from the body, individually packaged, then sealed in a brown bag. The samples were taken to the Bureau of Criminal Investigation (BCI) in Bowling Green. The tests did not immediately identify her.

The next step was Ancestral DNA, but that was costly and Sandusky did not have the money.

In the meantime, Wichman had retired, and Detective Eric S. Costante inherited the case. Deputy Marshal Bill Boldin connected Costante with *True Crime Garage* podcaster Nic Edwards, who is a board member of the Porchlight Project, a nonprofit that offers support to families of missing and murdered victims. The organization provides funds for DNA testing and genetic genealogy and works closely with Bode Technology. Edwards took the case to the rest of the Porchlight Project's board.

In November 2021, James Renner, the director of the Porchlight Project, emailed Costante that the organization was happy to foot the bill for the testing.

From there, Teresa Vreeland, the director of Forensic Genealogy Services of Bode, told Costante what samples to send. He packaged up the left and right femurs and the left and right hands with "crushed ends" and overnighted them to Bode's laboratory in Lorton, Virginia.

After DNA was extracted from the remains, Bode's Forensic Genealogy team went to work, combing public databases and other significant evidence and came up with a strong lead. The sample showed Jane Doe to be a full sibling to Raymond C. Geenwood Jr., who lived in Bay City, Michigan, and was one of twelve children. She was identified on March 30, 2023, exactly forty-three years from when she was found.

Detective Costante tracked down Raymond Greenwood Jr. and found out that he had a sister named Patricia Eleanore who was born in Bay City, but he had not seen or heard from her in many years.

Costante then located a surviving sister, Judy, who said she had not seen Patricia since the late '70s or early '80s when her sister lived with a man in Saginaw, Michigan. Judy said "Pat" came to her house with this man. She did not know his name, but she thought he looked like a pimp because he was dressed in bright red clothes. There were also three other men waiting out in the car. She told Costante she thought Patricia was a sex worker. She thought Pat was about thirty-two or thirty-four years old the last time she saw her. Judy told Costante that although her sister had a wild side, she did not think she had a police record.

The forensic genealogists found that Patricia was born on June 2, 1948, in Bay City, Michigan, to Raymond C. Greenwood Sr. (born in Little Current, Ontario, Canada) and Eleanore Kotewa (born in Bay City, Michigan).

A trip through Ancestry.com and the Archives of Michigan, Michigan History Center, by this author revealed that the couple first married in 1937 and later divorced. Raymond was sent to the Michigan State Prison at Jackson in 1938 for breaking and entering (nighttime). Eleanore married Floyd Adelbert Valentine. That marriage last two years. Raymond served two years and was paroled in 1940. He was discharged from parole three years after that. She and Raymond Sr. remarried in 1946. They had twelve children—eight boys and four girls.

Patricia did not have an easy life. At some point, the children's mother put all of them up for adoption. Judy said Patricia—her mother's favorite—was only twelve at the time. No one could understand why their mother did not keep Patricia with her. Patricia was very disturbed over being adopted out and never got over it. She suffered a nervous breakdown and even received electroshock treatments. She wound up in Traverse City after that. It is unknown why the children were adopted out. Detective Costante contacted Michigan Health and Human Services but found no records for foster care or adoption for the Greenwood family.

Both Patricia's sister and brother said she moved around frequently but did spend time with their oldest brother, Robert, who is now deceased. The family had no photos of Patricia or documents with personal information on them.

As of this writing, Detective Costante is waiting for a possible driver's license or state ID card from the Michigan State Police Department.

Did Patricia Eleanore Greenwood accidentally fall into the icy water of Lake Erie? Did she intentionally jump into those dark waters? Or did someone kill her and dispose of her body in the depths of the lake?

Sandusky police detective Eric Costante believes the latter and is treating the case as a homicide.

If you have any information or photos of Patricia Eleanore Greenwood, call Detective Costante at 419-627-5866.

8

WHO KILLED NANCY EAGLESON?

Wearing a black-and-white-checked dress with matching jacket and her very first pair of high heels, fourteen-year-old Nancy Eagleson set off with her five-year-old sister, Sheryl, hand in hand, to go to the movies. It was Sunday, November 13, 1960, and unseasonably warm, so the girls walked the ten or twelve minutes from their Klinger Road (now Flat Rock Drive) home to the Paulding Theater. *David and Bathsheba* was showing along with another movie. The film was probably above Sheryl's head. She was restless and finally fell asleep, but that was OK. She loved being with her big sister, and her sister loved being with her. The two were inseparable. Nancy was like a second mother to Sheryl.

After the show, the girls stopped for a soda at Johnson's restaurant, where they met some of Nancy's friends. It had been a fun outing for the girls, but it was getting close to 7:00 p.m. and time to go home. They did not know it would be the last day they would ever share.

As the evening wore on, Nancy's feet started to hurt in her new black leather heels, so she and Sheryl stopped by to see their father, Donald, at Wyatt's Bowling Alley. He worked full time at International Harvester across the state line in Fort Wayne but managed the bowling alley on weekends. Nancy asked her dad if he would run them home. He said he would if they could wait until the end of his shift.

Nancy did not want to wait, so she took her sister's hand, and the two started the six-block walk toward home.

Left: Fourteen-year-old Nancy Eagleson was abducted minutes from her home and later murdered that same evening. *Courtesy of the Eagleson family.*

Right: Nancy Eagleson took her sister Sheryl with her everywhere. *Courtesy of the Eagleson family.*

It was close to 7:30 p.m. and darkness was approaching, but the streets were well lighted as the girls headed down East Jackson and onto the wooden pedestrian walkway over the old iron bridge that crossed Flat Rock Creek. At the corner of Jackson and Klinger Roads, they cut through an abandoned gas station and started down the few blocks to their house. There were no sidewalks, so the girls kept to the side of the road.

Nancy and Sheryl were within six or seven houses of their home when a car came from behind them. Sheryl remembered the large, dark-colored car creeping up beside them. The driver, a man, cranked down his window and asked if they needed a ride. "No," Nancy told him firmly. "We are almost home." The man drove off.

Although Nancy and Sheryl would be home by themselves, the neighborhood was safe; Nancy was very responsible, and their mother, Bettie, who was working at Temple's Drive-in Restaurant, was only a half mile away.

Minutes later, the man came back and asked again. When Nancy said "no" the second time, he drove the car square in front of them, blocking their path. He flung open his door and stepped out. Before Nancy could react, he grabbed her and started dragging her toward the car.

According to Sheryl, as Nancy struggled against the man, he pulled something from his pocket, then yanked open the rear door and shoved Nancy into the back seat. The five-year-old tried to help her sister and jumped onto the man's back, but he hit her in the stomach and threw her down. As Sheryl looked up from the ground, she saw the car speed away going north on Klinger Road. She said Nancy's head was motionless against the back seat. It was the last time she would ever see her sister.

Sheryl ran to Betty and John Larson's house, close neighbors who had often watched her and her sister when their parents worked late. John immediately phoned the police.

Members of the Paulding Village Police Department, Paulding County Sheriff's Office and the girls' parents began a frantic hunt for the dark-colored car—maybe black, green or blue—that Sheryl described to Deputies

Nancy and Sheryl Eagleson went to the Paulding Theater to see *David and Bathsheba* the afternoon before Nancy was abducted and murdered. *Courtesy of the Eagleson family.*

Nancy Eagleson at Christmas
with a puppy and her sister
Sheryl on the left. *Courtesy of the
Eagleson family.*

Frank Shipman and Tom Rosselet. Throughout the ordeal, Sheryl described
Nancy's assailant as older than her father. He wore glasses, and his hair was
gray at the sides. He was wearing a suit and tie like he was going to church.
She said he smelled like alcohol. Police later suspected it was chloroform.

The search came to a devastating end around 2:30 in the morning
when two Paulding hunters, Joseph Aufrance, thirty-eight, and Kenneth
Nelson, forty-three, found Nancy's body seven miles from home. She was
lying in a secluded clearing in a heavily wooded area one hundred feet
off Paulding County Road Route 176 near Junction. The men had been
hunting racoons when they and their dogs happened across what at first
looked to them like a discarded Halloween costume. As they drew closer,
they saw she was mostly clothed except for her undergarments lying beside
her. Her head lay in a small pool of blood. Just as the hunters came out of
the woods, an Ohio State trooper, who had been canvasing the area, saw
them and stopped.

Nancy's body was found by two hunters in this wooded area seventy-five feet from the road. *Courtesy of the Eagleson family.*

Paulding, with only 2,300 citizens, had always been a quiet community with little serious crime. No one locked their doors, not even at night. The only other murder had happened six years before. Everyone in the village knew everyone else. They went to church together. They shopped in the same stores. Their children went to the same schools. Their kids rode their bikes in the streets until dark and played in the woods with little or no supervision. It was a safe town. The village had a small police department, and Paulding County Sheriff's Department had only three deputies plus Sheriff John L. Keeler.

The Eaglesons were friends with Keeler, and he knew Nancy quite well, as she had worked on his reelection campaign. Because of the county's low crime rate, he had never investigated a murder this horrendous. He knew he was going to need help and called in the Ohio State Police for assistance with the investigation.

The crime scene was never properly secured. The hunters with their dogs had walked around on the site. Along with police, locals and searchers arrived. Newspaper reporters got wind of it and showed up. With so much foot traffic, it would have been easy for evidence to be trampled, go unnoticed or be missed.

When asked about tire tracks at the scene, Keeler said there were too many leaves in the area, which would have covered any tracks. There was mention of a tree stump near the road with a scrape of paint on it, but no one thought to take a sample of the paint and no one remembers the color for certain.

Louis A. Schneider, MD, performed the autopsy on Monday, November 14, at Saint Joseph's Hospital in Fort Wayne, Indiana. Deputy Shipman identified the body at the coroner's office. Schneider found that Nancy had been shot under the left side of her chin, and there was an exit wound above her right eye. She had been beaten and raped. Schneider set the time of her death at approximately 9:00 p.m.

A semen sample, fingernail clippings, a bullet fragment (possibly .22 caliber) and evidence of a bloody fingerprint on Nancy's arm were turned over for the police file. Nancy's black-and-white-checked dress with matching jacket and her first pair of high heels were placed in the file, as were her scarf, bra, underwear, garter belt (with one of the clasps missing after the murder), hose, necklace, purse with a letter and money and hair from a tree branch at the scene. The forensic evidence was supposedly turned over to the Toledo crime lab, then stored in the old jail.

When the family returned home after learning of Nancy's death, they attempted to use the phone, but it did not work. Donald went to see why. It looked to him as though the line had been cut. With little Sheryl being the only witness who could identify Nancy's abductor, Don and Bettie feared for her safety and decided to leave their home. They went to stay at Bettie's parents' house.

Police began the investigation by questioning anyone and everyone from the Paulding community, especially if they had a dark-colored car. They followed up on every tip in the hopes of developing a lead, including information on a couple of outsiders who were acting strangely in local bars. Keeler compiled a "list of possible suspects," an official told the *Sandusky Register*.

"We also know thirty men who didn't do it," Sheriff Keeler told a reporter for the *Alliance Review*. Detectives had questioned thirty men, including known sex offenders in Northwestern Ohio, but dismissed them as suspects for one reason or another.

Calls continued to pour in. One of them seemed particularly interesting. It came from Frank Lienard of Antwerp, Ohio. He told police that a stranger had stopped at his house at 1:30 in the morning—just an hour before Nancy was found. He wanted directions to Kendallville, Indiana. Lienard was leery of the man because he acted strange. Lienard's house was a direct route toward Indiana from the wooded area where Nancy's body was found. He described the stranger as about 5'7" tall and weighing 155 pounds. The man had dark hair with some gray, and he wore glasses.

A few days after Nancy's death, the investigation began to settle on a seventeen-year-old former mental health patient, Robert Stovall.

The teenager was arrested east of LaPort, Indiana, and was being questioned in the death of Gloria Kowalewicz, a nine-year-old girl who had been snatched and killed in Chicago. There were similarities. Gloria was taken off the street as she walked to church. Her body was found in a wooded area, seventy-five feet off the road. She had been shot in the head twice with a .38-caliber gun. At the time, authorities thought Nancy had been shot once, possibly with a .22.

Although the slayings happened 230 miles and approximately eight hours apart, with Gloria dying first, Sheriff Keeler was interested in Stovall because of the similarities. The suspect was found sleeping in a stolen car by Indiana state trooper Clyde Lane. Lane saw blood on his trousers and the inside of the suspect's coat. He claimed the bloodstain had come from a bar fight in Detroit. He gave police several different stories during the interrogation. He contended that the car belonged to his sister, but he had neither registration for the car nor a driver's license. Police found out the car had been stolen in Chicago.

The teen told police he was from Montrose, Michigan, and that he worked as a mechanic at General Motors. In truth, he was from Jacksonville, Illinois. None of what he told them added up. His bloody clothing and samples of mud from his shoes were sent to the Chicago Crime Lab. Authorities showed a photo of the suspect to Sheryl, but she did not recognize him. The teenager was never charged with either murder.

Everyone in Paulding had an opinion on who the murderer might be. Some thought it was a predator driving through the area who just happened to see two young girls walking—a crime of opportunity. Others believed it was someone local. For one thing, the area where Nancy's body was found would have been known only to someone local.

Restaurant owner Virgil Johnson came to mind for those who thought it was a local man. Johnson was one of the last men, besides their father, to see the girls, and he knew they were walking home alone. Johnson was not aware of the rumors at first. Even his wife mentioned seeing blood in the back seat of his car and on his clothing. But Johnson explained that he owned a restaurant and often picked up meat from the butcher shops.

Left: Nancy with her mother, Bettie, and father, Donald. *Courtesy of the Eagleson family.*

Below: The Eagleson family. Nancy is in the lower left with her younger sister Sheryl next to her. *Courtesy of the Eagleson family.*

At one point, discussions about Johnson were getting heated, and Keeler thought the restaurateur might be in danger, so he took him to jail—not because he was a suspect, but for his safety. Johnson passed a lie detector test, and Keeler cleared him. Chances were Sheryl would have told police if Johnson, or anyone local, had abducted Nancy.

Joseph Aufrance was another local man considered by police. He lived close by the woods where he and Nelson found Nancy. Aufrance's daughter was friends with Nancy. He arrived home from the crime site that morning to change clothes and told his wife he thought he might be a suspect. Although he looked something like the police composite sketch, he was never arrested.

Nancy was born on July 3, 1946, and raised in Paulding, so her funeral services were held at the Paulding Church of Christ on November 17. It was the church she regularly attended and where she went to church camp. The Reverends Ray White and S. Glenn Cameron conducted the services. She was buried at Live Oak Cemetery. At least five hundred people paid their respects. Her friends and family remembered the petite, blue-eyed Paulding High School freshman with the light-brown hair and great sense of humor. Jeanne Windsor, a close friend and advocate for the family, told *Uncovered* how much Nancy loved jokes and loved to laugh. She even had a book where she recorded riddles, pranks and her favorite jokes.

In December, Prosecutor John F. DeMuth's office started a reward fund with $1,000 for information leading to the apprehension and conviction of Nancy's killer. The fund quickly grew to $5,000 with donations from Van Wert and Defiance F.O.P.s, the Knights of Columbus and two local unions. In the next few days, more money poured in from Veterans of Foreign Wars, the Paulding Volunteer Fire Department, businesses and citizens. The reward was spearheaded by Kenny Bryan and rose to $6,500. Clearly, Paulding wanted Nancy's killer caught.

In January, Sheriff Keeler began reaching out to other police and sheriff's departments. He found out about Thomas Ball, thirty, of Hicksville, who was a suspect in the assault and rape of a Butler, Indiana woman. Police also thought they could connect him to an attempt to pick up an Indiana girl. But the evidence as far as Paulding's case did not pan out.

Keeler thought Mark Hodges, who was reported drinking in a nearby bar around the time of Nancy's abduction, could be the man he was looking for. His intuition could have been right, because Hodges was later accused of two murders. He got off for those cases but was later sent to prison for sex crimes.

In an effort to get more information from Sheryl, police had her hypnotized three times. They even offered her a pony if she could remember more. She

Nancy Eagleson and her father, Donald. *Courtesy of the Eagleson family.*

was only five years old and most likely traumatized, but she did the best she could and gave enough information for a police artist to create a composite sketch.

Today, more than sixty years later, Sheryl's memories are fuzzy, but she remembers an attempted break-in at her grandmother's house. She was standing on a chair at the sink in the kitchen at the back of the house, helping Bettie do the dishes after the evening meal. Her mother left her for a moment to go give her grandmother some medicine. The weather was bad out, and the wind was rattling the windows. Sheryl was nervous being alone. All of a sudden, the back door flew open. Sheryl thought she saw someone standing in the doorway. She screamed. Bettie came running, but the person was gone. Bettie called Don, her father and the sheriff. They found where the door had been pried with either a knife or screwdriver that was left behind. There were also footprints in the snow that led to a nearby road.

The sheriff's report at the time seemed to downplay the event, implying that Bettie had overreacted. No mention of the footprints or the instrument used to force the door lock were in the report. However, Bettie explicitly remembered that the door had been tampered with and either a knife or screwdriver had been left behind. In recent times, Sheryl has spoken with someone who saw and followed the tracks in the snow.

Many years have passed, and justice has eluded the Eagleson family. Nancy's sister Merrill was born eleven months after the murder. Donald died in 1978.

In 1985, the Eagleson family discovered that Nancy's murder file, supposedly stored in the old jail, had come up missing. Nancy's clothing, as well as all the forensic evidence—semen specimens, fingernail scrapings, a hair sample from a tree limb and a bullet fragment—had disappeared with no explanation.

In 2007, the jail and sheriff's department were moved to a new location. In 2013, Jeff and Cassie Hollis, owners of All Trades Restoration Company, purchased the old 1874 jail and began renovations to turn it into a destination for haunted jail tours. While working in the basement, they found a small leather high-heeled shoe and a piece of cloth. Could they have belonged to Nancy?

Bettie looked at the shoe but could not be sure if it was Nancy's. Sheriff Jason K. Landers was elected in 2012 and still serves as sheriff. He called officials from the National Center for Missing and Exploited Children (NCMEC) that had investigated the case two years earlier. The Bureau of Criminal Investigation showed up with its vans. Technicians sifted through the dirt in the basement where the shoe was found, but nothing else turned up. They took the shoe back to their lab to test for DNA but could not obtain a profile.

Bettie died in 2018 without ever knowing who killed her daughter. She is buried close to Nancy.

In 2022, Sheryl and her sister, Merrill, wanted one last chance to get answers and justice for Nancy. It was a hard decision to make, but they decided to have Nancy's body exhumed. Jeanne Windsor was instrumental in helping attorney John DeMuth complete the paperwork to petition the Paulding County Court on their behalf. Since all the original evidence was gone, they hoped that a new autopsy might reveal DNA or some other evidence that could lead to the killer. Judge Michael Wehrkamp agreed and granted their petition.

The cost of disinterment and DNA testing was going to be high. The family started a GoFundMe website and hosted a public concert to raise money. The Porchlight Project, a nonprofit organization that offers support for families of the missing and murdered, provided the rest of the funds, according to the organization's founder and president James Renner.

On October 24, 2022, Nancy's remains were exhumed. Lucas County deputy coroner Thomas Blomquist, MD, PhD, performed the autopsy over a three-day period. He was assisted one day by forensic anthropology consultant Julie Saul. Blomquist found that Nancy had been shot twice in the head—not once, as the first autopsy had found. A deformed bullet was recovered under her head, but BCI determined it had no identifying features for forensic comparison. Some small fibers were found around one hip, but they were not tested, as the lab technicians felt they could have come from Nancy's clothing.

Merrill (*left*), the youngest sister, born after Nancy's death, and Sheryl, with their mother, Bettie. Though the photo label says "Betty," her obituary and other records spell it "Bettie." *Courtesy of the Eagleson family.*

Pulitzer Prize–winning WTOL 11 reporter Brian Dugger has spent countless hours investigating and writing about the Nancy Eagleson case. On one of his trips to Paulding, he had a conversation with Don Rhonehouse, who claimed to have witnessed Nancy's abduction. Although he did not give the make and model of the car, he told Dugger he knew the shape of it and its taillights and what the seats looked like. He said he could see a struggle in the car. At the time, he was driving a Corvair that could not keep up with the suspect car. He said he went to the sheriff's department that night, but deputies made no report.

Rhonehouse felt—as some others in the town did—that Sheriff Keeler, who died in 1986, tried to cover up the identity of the killer. Sheriff Landers did not know Keeler, but said, "It's alleged that he always kept his buddies and family out of trouble, but covering up for the abduction, rape, murder of a fourteen-year-old little girl just doesn't make sense."

During Dugger's interview with Rhonehouse, the Paulding man produced what looked like a .22-caliber gun and told Dugger he thought it was the murder weapon. He claimed someone at his sister's class reunion gave it to him. BCI took control of the gun. Both Rhonehouse and his sister were interviewed by authorities, but no new information was gained.

After more than half a century, there is still a commitment to solve this case. In addition to help from Dugger and the Porchlight Project, Uncovered.com, an online organization, has digitized Nancy's entire case file to make it easier for police to use. In February 2023, *Uncovered* hosted a web event, "Justice Delayed: A Renewed Effort to Solve the Nancy Eagleson Murder Case." *Uncovered* has the largest database of unsolved cases in the country. Nik Edwards of the *True Crime Garage* podcast and a board member of the Porchlight Project is also responsible for digging through the files, interviewing Paulding residents and presenting what he has learned on his podcast.

If the killer were still alive, he would be at least eighty if not older, and the evidence is gone.

Sheriff Landers recently said, "From my cold case review at the NCMEC years ago on this case, I believe it will take a 'deathbed confession' to wrap this up." He went on to say, "It would take a confession that is so articulate it matches all the facts written in the report from the first narrative." The confession would have to be "extremely articulate," he said, to satisfy Sheryl, her family and him.

9

MARION BRUBAKER'S MURDER UNSOLVED

The temperature in Akron was eighty degrees on August 27, 1962, down from previous days that reached up into the nineties—still hot, but a nice day for a bike ride. Summer was winding down, and school would be starting in a few weeks. Twelve-year-old Marion Brubaker would have been starting seventh grade at Lakeview School in September if someone had not murdered her on a shortcut through the trees only minutes from her home on Killian Road in Coventry Township.

Marion was an avid reader, and she spent her last few hours at the Portage Lake Branch of the Akron-Summit County Public Library on Manchester Road and took out young adult novels *Princess in Denim* by Zoa Sherburne, *Sue Barton, Visiting Nurse* by Helen Dore Boylston and *The Secret of the Martian Moons* by Donald A. Wollheim. Shortly after 3:00 p.m., she put the books in her bicycle's basket and left the library for the familiar three-mile ride home. The trip to the library was a frequent ride for the slim, 5'2", dark-haired girl. On her way home, she detoured to the Scott's drugstore in Coventry Plaza, where she bought a greeting card for her mother. Then she hopped back on her bike and headed for home.

As usual, she took the diagonal cutoff through a wooded area at the northeast corner of Main Street and Killian Road. It was a well-used shortcut through the trees that ended in a farmer's field just a few blocks from her house. But she would never make it out of those woods.

Twelve-year-old Marion Joyce Brubaker was attacked and killed near her home on Killian Road in 1962. *Cleveland Public Library Photo Collection.*

At 4:12 p.m., around the time that Marion was murdered, a sheriff's cruiser, its siren wailing, was on its way to an accident on Killian Road. It passed within a few hundred feet of Marion's body.

A fifteen-year-old boy happened to be in the woods at the same time and discovered Marion. He ran to his South Main Street home, which was directly across the street from the woods. "I think there's a dead girl up in the woods," he told his father. His father immediately called the sheriff's office.

According to the police report, the boy told his father about the body at 4:30 p.m. Four detectives were dispatched to the boy's home. The teenager took them across the street to the woods and to where he had found the girl and her bicycle. The detectives found blood, hair and pieces from a bottle approximately nine hundred feet inside the woods, indicating the spot where she may have been attacked. Her bike lay on its side under an apple tree with the library books and greeting card she had bought for her mother spilling out of its basket. Her pocketbook lay on the ground, as did her broken glasses.

Marion's lifeless body was located in a thicket forty feet off the path from where her bike was found. From the blood and marks in the path, detectives thought she had been dragged there. Her still-warm body was lying on her back. One of the deputies checked for a pulse, but there was none. Her body was nude from the waist down. According to an article by Phil Trexler in both the *Akron Beacon Journal* and the *Daily Herald*, her

Library books and a greeting card spilled out of Marion Brubaker's bicycle basket when she was attacked. *From the* Akron Beacon Journal, *USA Today Network.*

red-checkered shorts were torn and her underwear was inside out. Both articles were flung across her face, hiding her still-open eyes. Profilers often think this could mean shame, remorse or a relationship to the victim. Her shirt and bra were pulled up to her chin. Her tennis shoes and socks were left next to her body.

There were bruises on her neck, leading deputies to believe she had been strangled. Scratches on her body indicated she had put up a frantic fight and that she had possibly been dragged from her bicycle to the thicket. She had a cut on the back of her head, and deputies thought she may have been hit with the broken bottle found by her bicycle.

At first, detectives thought she had been raped. Summit County coroner William J. Pittenger found during the autopsy that was not the case, but detectives believed that the motive was sexual assault. Strangulation was ruled as the cause of death, and the time of death was perhaps forty minutes before detectives got there.

One of the detectives found a library card in one of the books. It had Marion's name and address on it. Two of the deputies went to the address on the card to inform her parents. Her shaken father, the Reverend Clair Brubaker, returned with the deputies to identify her.

Marion was the daughter of Brubaker and his wife, Ruth. Marion loved music and played the piano and sang. The night before she died, she and one of her three sisters sang a duet at the Hillwood Chapel Community Church, where her father was the pastor. She also led a Bible training group at church. She was a quiet girl, studious and an excellent student at school. She thought she would like to become a teacher.

Her father told reporters she was "a fine Christian girl." He spoke for his wife and daughters Martha, Evelyn and Nadine when he said, "We have prayed and settled everything here in the family."

Services for Marion were held on Thursday, August 30, at the Hillwood Chapel Community Church. She was buried in the Hillside Memorial Park Cemetery on Canton Road. According to one report by WKYC, at least six hundred people attended.

The fifteen-year-old boy who found Marion seemed cooperative when he led the detectives into the woods and showed them where he had found the dead girl, but something did not seem right.

As far as they could tell, he was the only person besides Marion in the woods that day. They asked what he was doing in there. The Coventry High School freshman answered that he was bored, so he decided to take a walk.

First, he showed them the bicycle with a purse and the books. He said he looked through them but then continued on his walk. When he came to the field he stepped out and saw a man on a tractor. He and the man looked at each other, but then the youth turned around and went back into the woods. He told investigators that was when he discovered the girl's body.

Apparently, they did not believe him because they took him into the sheriff's department, where he endured hours of grilling. The first question they asked him was if he knew Marion Brubaker. He told them no. But they knew better. They knew he and she had gone to the same school. When faced with that fact, he admitted he did know her. They quizzed the boy about a campsite with a chair and a girly magazine they had discovered in the woods. He confessed to looking at the magazine but denied it was his. They eyed scratches on his hand. What about those, they asked. The 5'10", two-hundred-pound teenager claimed to not remember how he got them. Detectives noted that there were no fingerprints on the bicycle or the books except for a partial print on the handlebar and print on one of the books. The teenager finally admitted that he had wiped the surfaces of her bike, pocketbook and the books after he had found her, sorry that he had handled them when he first saw them. According to *Beacon Journal* writer Mark Price in an article published on the fiftieth anniversary of Marion's death, fourteen Akron police officers were helping the sheriff's department with the investigation. They had the physical evidence sent to the FBI Criminal Laboratory in Quantico, Virginia, but no useable prints were found.

Although sheriff's detectives were most suspicious of the youth who found Marion, they also looked at vagrants and men with records. They picked up a thirty-six-year-old man found wandering around the South Main Street area on Tuesday, the day after the murder, and questioned him over a day and a half. They asked him about the campsite in the woods and the magazine. He freely admitted that the magazine belonged to him. He also told them he had seen the girl on a bicycle in the woods, but he did not know where she was headed. The vagrant told interrogators that he saw a man on a tractor when he momentarily stepped out of the woods. The farmer, who owned the field at the entrance to the woods, remembered seeing only one person come out to the clearing that day, but he could not tell if it was the boy or the man. One report said the person was wiping his forehead. The vagrant took a lie detector test and was released on Wednesday morning.

Detectives quizzed two or three other men and released them. Other teenage boys from close by were questioned, according to a source. One person who was interrogated extensively in Marion's murder was a nineteen-year-old man who was a parole violator for a previous felony conviction. He had no record of sex offenses, and investigators did not think he was involved.

Authorities questioned known sex offenders in the area, but they continued to focus on the bespectacled fifteen-year-old boy who said he found Marion's body. They were suspicious of his changing stories, and according to a Cleveland.com article that cited court records, the buttons were torn off from his shirt and the zipper on his pants was broken and partially down. And then there were those scratches on his right hand that he did not remember where or how he had gotten them. No mention was made about how fresh they looked. The dark, wavy-haired teen was held and interrogated all that Monday evening and up until early the next morning. His clothing and fingernails were examined, but they yielded no evidence. Detectives caught him lying, but he denied killing Marion. One of the sheriff's detectives told the *Plain Dealer* that the teen was "caught in some obvious lies but still denies murdering the girl." Results from the boy's lie detector test on the night of Marion's murder were inconclusive. When Akron police investigators took a look at the case fifty years later, they found the teen had actually failed three polygraphs and that Sheriff Robert Campbell had the boy removed from the station during the polygraph.

The youth was released sometime after that.

At first, both Campbell and Assistant County Prosecutor George Pappas thought the boy was guilty, but they had no solid evidence. In spite of the lack of evidence, they had him picked up again a couple of weeks later.

Near the end of September, the prosecutor took the matter before juvenile court judge Russell Thomas. In addition to accusing the youth of giving false information to the authorities, Pappas told Judge Thomas that the teen had tried to molest one of his sister's girlfriends on more than one occasion, including once in the wooded area where Marion's body was found. Pappas also told the judge that the boy said he had wanted to kill someone to see what it was like.

The youth's attorney, George Hargreaves, conceded that the prosecutor's statements were true with the exception of a claim that the boy had said he wanted to see what it was like to kill someone.

The judge ruled the boy delinquent and ordered psychological and diagnostic testing under the juvenile court's jurisdiction. The fifteen-year-old was then sent to the Juvenile Detention Home, where Dr. Norman Bills, director of psychological testing services, assessed him. Bills said he learned a lot about the boy as a person but nothing about the Marion Brubaker case.

The boy was released from custody and briefly placed with his grandmother in Waverly, West Virginia, but later brought home to his parents in Summit County. He was never charged with Marion's murder because Pappas did not think the evidence was sufficient. Later on, Pappas came to question whether the boy was even guilty. He felt Campbell concentrated on the boy right off the bat when the investigation should have been broader.

Also, in September, Summit County commissioner John Poda proposed a resolution to the county board of commissioners to offer a $1,000 reward for information leading to the arrest and conviction of Marion's murderer. The resolution passed. The reward was contingent on the indictment of the guilty person. Private donors were encouraged. A panel composed of the sheriff, county prosecutor and the trial judge would decide whether the source was entitled to the reward. All law enforcement personnel were excluded from participating in the reward. The resolution was set to expire on January 1, 1964.

According to an *Akron Beacon Journal* account in December 2020 written by Paula Schleis and Stephanie Warsmith, a promising tip came in to retired deputy Thomas Anderson in March 1964. Anderson was running for sheriff against Campbell and had accused Campbell of not following up on the tip. Sheriff's investigators had spent nineteen months on the case. Investigators had interviewed or questioned more than one hundred people and administered polygraphs to some of the more likely subjects, but Campbell claimed to be unaware of the lead.

The tip came via an employee of the Greyhound Bus Terminal and involved a peddler named William Lewis, who hung around the bus station. Lewis told a ticketing agent that he had seen a girl's body in the woods on the same day Marion was murdered.

Campbell said he had never heard of Lewis, but he had him tracked down and pulled in for questioning on March 3.

Forty-nine-year-old William James Lewis was a slightly built man who went door to door selling potholders. Although he was picked up near his rooming house in Canton, he originally lived on Main Street in Hubbard in Trumbull County. His sister lived in Akron, and he visited her on occasion.

At first, Lewis denied killing Marion, but after three days of intense questioning without a lawyer present, he confessed. He said he had seen her many times in her yard when he was on his way to his sister's house. So, when he saw her in the woods, he ran after her and tried to talk to her. When he pushed her off her bike, she fell and struck her head on a rock, he said. Right after that, he strangled her because he was afraid that she would tell her father he had hit her. Then he heard a police siren, so he quickly hid the bike and ran to his sister's house half a mile away. The

Marion Joyce Brubaker was laid to rest at the Hillside Memorial Park Cemetery on Canton Road. *Photo by Jane Ann Turzillo*

police cruiser, on its way to an accident, passed within two hundred yards of the wooded path.

Lewis told authorities he confessed because God told him to "tell the truth." He said he felt much better after confessing. When he spoke with reporters, who were given permission to question him, he told them he confessed because his "conscious" (not conscience) bothered him.

A *Plain Dealer* article said he was illiterate and capable of writing only his name, so he confessed into a Dictaphone.

Deputies took Lewis to the woods, where he described what had happened that day, but they learned nothing new. Everything Lewis shared had already been in the media.

Ten days later, Lewis confessed to killing twelve-year-old Ruth Guthrie of Tallmadge on June 12, 1963. He claimed to have buried her body in a wooded area near Emmit Road, off Route 91 in Tallmadge. Police departments from Tallmadge, Stow and Cuyahoga Falls along with Summit County deputies searched the area using a mine detector and a bulldozer, but no body was found. After that, Lewis repudiated his confession in Ruth's murder. When he went before the judge a few days later to be arraigned in Barberton Court on first-degree murder charges for Marion's case, he was with an attorney, and he recanted his confession.

Investigators found Lewis had a history of mental illness. Summit County Probate Court had adjudged him insane in 1945, and he had also been a patient at the Hawthornden State Hospital.

In May 1964, psychiatrists at Lima State Hospital found Lewis insane. He was kept at the Lima hospital. A Summit County grand jury refused to indict him.

After that, the case went cold.

Then, in October 2012—fifty years after Marion was murdered—Summit County sheriff's detectives Larry Brown and Joe Storad dusted off the case files. DNA technology was evolving, and they hoped it might provide some answers. They did not release many details to the media, but while reexamining the evidence, they found that Marion's fingernails had not been clipped or scraped during the autopsy, even though it was common practice to collect scrapings, blood, fibers and other forensic materials at the time. If Marion had fought her killer, she may have had skin or blood under her fingernails that if tested could lead to the killer. Detective Brown asked Summit County prosecutor Sherri Bevan Walsh to petition the court to have Marion's body exhumed.

According to Cleveland.com, court records on November 6, 2012, showed that Walsh and Summit County medical examiner Lisa Kohler issued the order to have Marion's body exhumed and a second autopsy performed.

The Reverend Clair D. Brubaker died in 2010. His wife, Ruth K. Brubaker, died in 2002. Their graves are close to Marion's. *Photo by Jane Ann Turzillo.*

This time, authorities were looking for scrapings from Marion's fingernails, as well as possible fibers from the fifteen-year-old's shirt that had been kept in evidence. Forensic evidence found in the second autopsy was sent to the Bureau of Criminal Investigation in Richfield.

After the samples were sent to BCI, detectives decided it was time to pay a visit to the original suspect, who in 2014 was sixty-seven years old. He had married and was living a law-abiding life. When detectives tried to talk with him, he refused to answer questions without an attorney present. He insisted on his innocence and would not take another polygraph.

The results of the fingernail scraping were disappointing. Marion's fingers did not hold the DNA or the answers as to who her killer was. And so, at this writing, more than sixty years have passed without knowing who took Marion Brubaker's life on that hot summer day of August 27, 1962.

10
TRIPLE MURDER IN ERIE COUNTY

Milan, Ohio, is a historic village of just over 1,300 people. It is best known for the birthplace of Thomas Edison, who was behind the invention of the incandescent light bulb, phonograph and alkaline battery. Sitting on the Erie and Huron County lines, it is an all-American town, a rural, quiet and normally peaceful place to live.

That peace was shattered in 1968 with the gruesome triple murder of William and Ann Cassidy and their daughter, twelve-year-old Patricia. The Cassidys also had a seventeen-year-old son, Michael, who was working and not at home when his family was slain. A one-year-old black pup named Maggie, who slept on the back porch, rounded out the family.

The home in Milan, where the family had lived for eight years, was outside of town on State Route 13 (at the time SR 299), a quarter mile from the Ohio Turnpike. The Norfolk & Western Railroad tracks also ran close by. Their two-story, seven-room farmhouse was attractive. It was white with green trim and was isolated by surrounding cornfields. A small barn stood out back. Having lived there for eight years, they felt safe enough to never lock their doors. They trusted people, a relative told the *Lorain Journal*.

In the early hours of Monday, April 1, 1968, William, Ann and Patty, as she was called, were sleeping in their bedrooms on the second floor when someone probably picked up the family's 12-gauge shotgun, which was left on the back porch, entered the house, went upstairs and fired bullets into William and Ann and bludgeoned Patty.

Forty-one-year-old William was originally from Detroit, Michigan. His family moved to Huron, where his father became the mayor at one point. William was a navy veteran from World War II. He had owned Cassidy Supply Company, a safety equipment business, when the family lived in Huron. At the time of his death, he was working as a diesel pump operator at U.S. Steel construction in Lorain.

He was shot twice point-blank with a shotgun, once in the head, which took off part of the left side of his face, and once in the chest. He was dead at the scene.

Ann, his thirty-seven-year-old wife, was originally from Berlin Heights, Ohio. She worked as the morning barmaid at Andy's & Willy's Tavern in Huron.

She had also been shot in the head with a round that nearly took the top of her head off. She was clinging to life when found.

Patty was a seventh grader and a member of the school choir. She loved kittens and had several. She was responsible enough to babysit for one of her mother's best friend's children, who lived nearby. She was close to her older brother, Michael, because he always looked after her while their parents were working.

Hovering near death and lying across her bed, she had been beaten about the head. Police believed her assailant used the stock of the shotgun to bludgeon her into unconsciousness.

Michael Cassidy worked two part-time jobs. His first job was at Bill & Woody's Gulf Service Station on Cleveland Road West at Williams Street in Huron. Bill Smith, the manager there, told the *Morning Journal*'s reporter that Michael worked until one o'clock on Monday morning, April 1.

Smith spoke highly of the teen. He told the *Morning Journal* that Michael "is one of the finest kids I've ever had….If I could find four or five more like him today, I'd hire 'em all."

The boy's second job was at Andy's & Willy's Tavern (where his mother worked) at the corner of Main and Cleveland Road West in Huron. His duty there was to clean up after the tavern closed at 2:00 a.m. "He is the sweetest kid you could ever meet in your life. He took to me like a father," said Paul Shamhart, who worked at the tavern. He told the newspaper, "He's a damn good worker…never took a drink in his life—strictly soda pop." Shamhart also said Michael's parents got along "beautifully."

Although Michael was only seventeen, his mother had given him permission to work that late. After these two late-night jobs, he would sleep for only four hours before going school.

According to the current Erie County sheriff Paul Sigsworth, who is knowledgeable about the case, Michael clocked in at the tavern around 3:00 a.m. but was not there long.

Michael went home sometime after this and found his parents had been shot in their bed and his sister beaten about the head.

The seventeen-year-old panicked and drove about three miles to an ex-girlfriend's house. The girl's father called the Milan police. Although the Milan Police Department did not have an officer on duty overnight, Milan patrolman James Knally got the call at his home and drove to the Cassidy residence, where he met Michael. According to the initial Erie County sheriff complaint report, Knally radioed at 4:02 a.m. from the crime scene requesting a deputy. The coroner, Dr. Joseph Buder; the prosecutor, George Steinemann; Chief Deputy "Web" Beier; and Sergeant Harold Gladwell were all called to the Cassidy home. Deputy Lenke took Michael back to the station, where he was accompanied by an attorney sent by family members. He was interviewed by Steinemann, Sheriff Albert Hess and Sergeant Gladwell and was later released.

Ann and Patty were rushed to Fisher-Titus Memorial Hospital in Norwalk, where Ann died at 5:15 a.m., just fifteen minutes after arrival. The attending doctor said she had died due to "lacerations and contusions of the frontal area of the skull secondary to shotgun blasts to the frontal skull."

Patty was transferred to Elyria Memorial Hospital, where she underwent a five-hour brain surgery. It was reported that it took ninety-seven stitches to close the wounds she had suffered. The doctors gave her a fifty-fifty chance of surviving, but she never regained consciousness and died three days later.

The only witness left alive was Maggie, the Cassidy dog. She had gone missing but was found the day after the murders with an injury to her hindquarters. While one source claimed the dog was injured by the murderer, the *Morning Journal* reported that Michael said she had been hit by a car weeks before.

Erie County sheriff Hess said his deputies began the search for a 12-gauge shotgun—most likely the Cassidys' own shotgun that was usually kept on the back porch and was found missing. The sheriff called out a team to drag a nearby farmer's pond, while divers searched the bottom of the Huron River. They searched the water beneath Milan Bridge and Fries Landing but found nothing. The coast guard used grappling hooks to drag the bottom of the river under the big bridge at Huron.

The gun's barrel has never been found. They did find a shotgun shell casing. According to *Uncovered: Eye on Justice Investigates*, the casing was found near the kitchen door.

In the meantime, the township residents were nervous because no one had been arrested for the gruesome crime. People began to make sure their doors were locked and bolted at night. They kept their car doors locked. They adopted dogs for protection, kept loaded guns close at hand and began calling the sheriff's department every time they saw a stranger.

Although the sheriff assigned six men to the investigation, his department was stretched thin. "You can't be anyplace else," he said. "I don't have any more men." Although he said he had qualified people to handle the investigation, he realized he needed help. He asked for and got help from the Bureau of Criminal Investigation.

Crime scene agents from BCI spent two hours searching the Cassidys' home. They took the spent shotgun shell casing with them back to their lab to be checked for latent fingerprints. Investigators also found splinters of what looked to be part of a gunstock next to Patty's bed. Authorities would not reveal when, but they did find the rest of the stock out in the field behind the house. BCI agents also took with them some large pop bottles, a pair of dungarees (with no blood on them) and some other items that were not disclosed. The significance of the pop bottles and dungarees was not made public.

In looking over the case in March 2021, Vinnie Politan of *Court TV's Unsolved: The Cassidy Family Massacre* spoke with Sheriff Sigsworth and asked about the family. "They seemed to be a regular family. People in the community at that time were shocked and stunned by the fact that these individuals were murdered apparently in their sleep at night in their home."

Sigsworth said the records showed that the family was well thought of, and everything seemed normal. "There was nothing compelling that seemed to indicate that there was any type of problem between the family and other people in the community."

Investigators were stumped. They could not find the gun barrel. There did not seem to be a motive. The family had no enemies. There was no forced entry. There were no signs of resistance. Nothing had been taken, so it was not a burglary.

Sheriff Hess considered the possibility that it could have been a drifter off one of the trains that passed behind the Cassidys' property. He also wondered if it could have been someone off the turnpike, since it was not far away.

Deputies found Truman Capote's *In Cold Blood*, a 1966 best-selling true crime book, lying on the coffee table in the living room. The book is about the 1959 murder of four members of the Clutter family in rural Holcomb, Kansas. At first, they wondered if the killer had left the book there as if it was meant to be some kind of message. Hess even sent a couple of his men to see the movie, which had just come out in theaters the year before. Current sheriff Sigsworth told Court TV's Vinnie Politan that it was Ann's book, and she had been reading it.

Michael went to live with his grandmother Dorothy L. Hahn in Huron and attended the funerals of his mother, father and little sister. The star football player and popular senior went back to school a few days later. He commuted from Huron to Milan High School but "was having difficulty adjusting," his grandmother said. Mrs. Hahn said he had taken the deaths hard.

Law enforcement turned an eye toward Michael. Sandusky's Gerald H. Howells, who was Michael's attorney, told the *Morning Journal* that the teenager was cooperative and wanted to help find who killed his family. Two days after the murders, the teen was taken to Toledo for an hour-long lie detector test. Howell, as well as two of his relatives, two deputies and the prosecutor were present. The newspaper said the test "exonerated him from involvement in the slayings"; however, the sheriff later said, "It was a good test, but not conclusive."

Erie County prosecutor Steinemann was not convinced. In May, he said he wanted to hold a hearing in order to question Michael under oath. Michael's attorney objected to the proceeding, saying Steinemann was trying to lay a foundation to prosecute the youth. The attorney said Michael was not required to participate. The question went before Erie County Common Pleas Court judge James McCrystal. A week before the hearing, McCrystal ruled that Michael did not have to answer Steinemann's questions in the hearing. When the hearing commenced in July, Michael followed his attorney's advice and gave only his name and address when questioned.

The family's home was sold in December. A year after the murders, Michael joined the navy. The *Morning Journal* reported that investigators determined that he "was not involved" with the murders. Upon separation from the service, he moved out of state.

"Times have changed. Techniques have changed," Sigsworth said of the more than fifty years since the triple murder. "Things are done tremendously different than what was done in 1968....They did call for state crime scene agents to respond to the house." He believed they came a few days later. "Everybody did the best that they could," he said. Today, crime scene agents would come to the scene almost immediately to process evidence at the scene. "It just didn't happen then."

If anyone has any information about the murders of William, Ann and Patricia Cassidy, please call the Erie County Sheriff's Office at 419-625-7951.

11

END OF WATCH

Conspiracies and speculation have swirled around the death of Rock Creek police chief Robert Hamrick since his high-speed chase ended in an accident in the early morning hours of March 11, 1970. Since that tragic morning, the lines between fact and rumor have been blurred in news accounts and on social media. The case drew interest from the television series *Unsolved Mysteries*, filmed in 1991, and more recently by podcasts *Ohio Mysteries* and *Trace Evidence*.

Surrounded by farmland and wooded areas, Rock Creek is a small community that sits in south-central Ashtabula County. In 1970, it had a population of approximately five hundred. It was a quiet, peaceful town with one stoplight, a town hall, a library and other small businesses.

Things changed for the village in the late 1960s when a group of young toughs began to disrupt the peace. They harassed the citizens, got into bar brawls and operated a chop shop for stolen cars coming out of Cleveland.

Andrew A. Ceder, police chief of neighboring Jefferson Village, told *Unsolved Mysteries*, "They [the gang] were involved in fights. They were involved in threats. They had the entire village under their thumb. When they spoke, the village pretty much listened."

At the time, Rock Creek was patrolled by the Ashtabula County Sheriff's Department. With a little over 1,300 square miles, 740 of them county roads, deputies were stretched thin, so the village's Mayor David Schlecht established a police department in the hopes of putting a stop to the Rock

NORTHERN OHIO COLD CASES

Creek Gang's crime wave. The sheriff's department still dispatched calls, and deputies backed up the new police officers when needed.

Twenty-nine-year-old Robert Gilbert Hamrick was the third police chief to be appointed within a six-month period. His two predecessors resigned after being harassed and threatened by the gang. Hamrick swore the oath in July 1969 in front of his wife, Myrtle, and his three small children: Kenneth, six, Kris, two, and Brenda Sue, eight months.

Born in Widen, West Virginia, the new young chief had greenish-brown eyes, and he bore tattoos on his left arm and hand. He had not had an easy life and had not told Mayor Schlecht much about it. According to Ohio State Reformatory Historical Code of Conduct records located on the Ohio History Connection Archives/Library microfilm, his parents divorced when he was about seven, and he went to live with his grandparents. At age fourteen, with only a seventh-grade education, he struck out on his own. He worked as a farmhand at times and eventually joined the U.S. Army.

In 1961, he and three other men robbed another man of twenty-three dollars in neighboring Jefferson Village. He pleaded guilty and was sent to the Ohio State Reformatory at Mansfield in February of that year. His sentence was one to twenty-five years, but he was paroled on January 16, 1963, and came back to Ashtabula County. He turned his life around and a few years later joined the Geneva-on-the-Lake Police Department, according to an August 20, 2001 article in the *Star Beacon*.

Perhaps Hamrick's past made him more determined to stand up to the thugs. At 6'1" and 180 pounds, he was not so easily frightened or bullied.

Myrtle told *Unsolved Mysteries* that her husband wanted Rock Creek to be a nice, friendly town. He wanted to get the gang off the streets so people would not have to be afraid.

Less than a month after being sworn in, Hamrick served an arrest warrant for one of the local bad boys, Danny Smith (not his real name), for assault and battery on a Dorset individual. Around 8:30 p.m. on August 6, 1969, Hamrick found Smith at the Rock Creek Tavern. The two talked about the warrant, and Smith promised he would report to Hamrick the next morning and go to court with him. Hamrick warned Smith not to cause any trouble that night.

But later that evening, the sheriff's office received a complaint from Smith's assault victim. Apparently, Smith had been threatening him and throwing stones at his house. When Hamrick was notified, he searched for Smith at the Rock Creek Tavern, the Hunter's Tavern, Smith's apartment and other places he was known to frequent. When Hamrick did not find

Smith, he enlisted his friend, Patrolman Gary Martin, to help him in the hunt. Hamrick and Martin patrolled, looking for their man until 2:00 a.m. A third patrolman, James Watt, joined them in his own car. At one point, Smith sped past them as they sat at a gas station. They gave chase, but Hamrick's police car was not fast enough to catch Smith's 1959 black Ford, and they lost sight of him.

They went back to Martin's house and got his 1968 Pontiac GTO. Hamrick slapped the police department's magnetic signs on the sides of the Pontiac and used the red pursuit light from his car. Martin was behind the wheel. Somewhere along the line, Watt jumped in the car with them. When Smith came back into the village, they were ready.

Smith led them on a high-speed chase, reaching in excess of ninety miles per hour, up and down Water Street, Jefferson Avenue and High Street, sliding through turns and crashing a red light at Route 45. At that point, the GTO was close behind the Ford. Headed south, both cars drove down into a dip. Just as Smith's Ford came to the top of the dip, Hamrick fired three warning shots over the top of the Ford in an attempt to scare him into stopping. Smith drove another quarter of a mile and finally pulled over. His passenger had been hit with one of Hamrick's bullets, which entered the trunk lid and traveled through the back seat and struck the passenger.

The passenger, who was on leave from the military, was taken to Warren General Hospital in Trumbull County, where doctors said there was no serious damage. Smith was carted off to jail. Trumbull County Sheriff's Department sent a deputy to take the wounded passenger's statement, but he refused to talk to the deputy because of his dislike for Hamrick.

On January 31, 1970, while Hamrick was making a routine check of the abandoned Laird Lumber Building on Station Street, he came across a 1969 Stingray Convertible inside the building. A check on the license plate through the Bureau of Motor Vehicles revealed it had been reported stolen from Mentor on Christmas Eve. He and Patrolman Martin set up surveillance on the building and hid inside. At 12:30 p.m. the following day, a green pickup with two men inside rolled up to the building. The truck was towing a portable engine hoist. One of the men got out of the truck and unlocked the front door, walked through the building and opened the garage doors in the back. Hamrick and Martin watched the men unhook the hoist, bring it inside and wheel it to the front of the stolen car. One of the men then backed the truck inside the building and closed the door.

The two policemen overheard one of the men ask the other if he wanted "the radiator." The second man said "yes." The two unloaded their tools and began working on the Corvette, at which time Hamrick and Martin emerged from their hiding place and identified themselves. They arrested the two suspects for possession of a stolen vehicle. The men insisted they had not stolen the car. One of the subjects gave Hamrick and Martin the story that he had met a man in a bowling alley, but he did not know the man's name. The man said he had an engine, transmission and bucket seats for sale. They settled on a suspiciously low price, and the man gave him the location of the car and the combination to the front door lock on the building.

Mentor Police took the two in for questioning but released them back to Hamrick later in the day. Hamrick lodged them in the Ashtabula County Jail.

Prior to this arrest, gang members harassed Hamrick and his family. They would come by his house to taunt him. His wife told *Unsolved Mysteries* that he would get fed up and chase after them. One threat was most concerning. It came by telephone when Hamrick was not home. Myrtle answered the phone, and an unknown male voice on the other end told her Hamrick better leave things alone and get out of town, "or he's going to be hurt and hurt bad." But Hamrick was not intimidated. He stayed on the job until the early morning on March 11, 1970—his last day as Rock Creek's police chief.

The Ashtabula County Sheriff's radio log shows nothing unusual during that first bitter-cold hour of Wednesday, March 11, 1970. Deputy Michael Dispenza was the dispatcher. Each patrol car was known on the radio as an A for Ashtabula plus a number. Hamrick was A-5.

Deputy David F. Silva (A-15) arrested a drunk. Corporal William K. Johnston (A-17), who later became Sheriff Johnston, served a warrant. He was the supervisor for the sheriff's department during that shift. Deputy Dennis Chapman (A-11) did a sales check at the Pyma Valley Lounge. Police performed "sales checks" to make sure there were no liquor violations, such as underage drinking. They made sure the bars closed on time and that there was no alcohol consumption after hours.

At 12:56 a.m., Chief Hamrick (A-5) radioed dispatcher Dispenza that he was out of service for a sales check on the Rock Creek Tavern. Twenty-one minutes later, the chief was back on patrol. After that, Johnston, Chapman and a third deputy checked an open door at French's Mill. Silva reported a drunk to Ashtabula city police.

At 1:50 a.m., Chief Hamrick came over the radio, his siren screaming in the background, and informed Dispenza that he was in pursuit of a Chevrolet (later to be found a Javelin Rambler) southbound on Route 45. One minute later, he radioed that he was pursuing the car turning west on

Callender Road. That was the last time Chief Robert Hamrick (A-5) was heard from.

Akron Beacon Journal reporter Linda Frederick interviewed retired Deputy Chapman at the time *Unsolved Mysteries* looked into Hamrick's death. Chapman said he was thirty miles away when he first heard the radio transmission of the high-speed chase. He started out to back up Hamrick but got involved in a minor accident along Route 322 in Williamsfield Township and had to wait for the Ohio State Highway Patrol to take an accident report. Once he was freed up from his own accident at 3:02 a.m., he resumed patrol, probably thinking Hamrick's chase was over.

A half hour later, Dispenza radioed Chapman. The radio log read "Check Callender Rd. for A-5. Haven't heard from him or been able to contact him since 1:51 A.M. He had a high-speed chase going west on Callender Rd. from Rt. 45."

At first, Chapman assumed the chief had had car trouble and was stranded. But when he turned down the dark, ice-slick Callender Road, he found something else had happened.

As he drove out of a double S curve west on Callender Road, about 1,200 feet east of Windsor-Mechanicsville Road in Hartville Township, his headlights caught the reflection of the police department's shield off the side of Hamrick's cruiser. According to Dispenza's radio log, Chapman called in the accident at 3:43 a.m. "Callender Rd. 3 or 4 miles west of Rt 45. Send a sig.(nal) 29 (ambulance) and sig. 31 (tow truck). A-5 is up a tree."

Chapman wrote in his report that it looked as though Hamrick had lost control of the 1968 Dodge four-door cruiser on the slick, curving gravel road and had slammed into a tree. The cruiser was sitting approximately twelve feet from the edge of the road off the south side. The left front end of the cruiser hit the tree so hard that the car bounced backward. The emergency lights were off, and the light toggle switch was in the off position. The key in the ignition was broken off. Corporal Johnston later confirmed this.

Chapman found no footprints in the snow around Hamrick's cruiser, but there were deep skid marks leading up to the crash.

The driver's side door was jammed shut, so Chapman went to the passenger door and found Chief Hamrick in the front seat, half sitting, half lying between the seat and the steering wheel. His feet were on the passenger side of the drive shaft. As always, he was not wearing his seat belt.

Right away, Chapman could tell Hamrick was in serious condition. Hamrick was unconscious with head and facial injuries and had lost a lot of blood. However, Chapman later recalled the chief was semiconscious and

The corner of Windsor-Mechanicsville and Calender Roads. Hamrick crashed on a curve a quarter mile east. *Photo by Susan Hill.*

moving around in the front seat, possibly seizing. Chapman did not possess the medical skills to help Hamrick, so he radioed for an ambulance and wrecker at 3:45 a.m. Then he covered Hamrick with a blanket in an effort to make him comfortable until the ambulance arrived.

Johnston arrived at the accident scene at 4:00 a.m. He quickly assessed Hamrick's condition. "The Chief's head was a mass of blood and he had a swelling of the facial area. The chief was gasping for air, and it sounded like he had an open chest wound, further checking revealed that he did not have an open chest wound, he was still gasping for air," his report read.

When Miller Ambulance Service arrived, the two deputies helped the med team get Hamrick out of the car. The blanket Chapman had placed over him "fell to the ground, leaving a large blood spot in the snow," Johnston noted on his report. The blood in the snow would later add to speculation.

At 4:14 a.m., the ambulance left the scene with Johnston to clear the way, using full lights and sirens. He radioed Dispenza to have another cruiser (possibly Silva) block Routes 45 and 20 for the ambulance to pass and to ask Ashtabula city police to help block the roads into the city.

Severe curves headed west on Callender Road as Hamrick pursued a car at a high speed and lost control of his A-5. *Photo by Susan Hill.*

On March 11, 1970, Hamrick turned off Route 45 onto Callender Road south of Rock Creek on a doomed high-speed chase. *Photo by Susan Hill.*

The ambulance arrived at Ashtabula General Hospital at 4:36 a.m. An orderly at the hospital told Johnston that Hamrick was in "very serious condition."

Rumors started almost immediately, among them that Hamrick's gun and nightstick were missing from the wreck. According to Johnston's report of the investigation, a hospital orderly handed him Hamrick's pistol, holster, handcuffs, belt and a ring of keys at 5:20 a.m.

In the meantime, Myrtle Hamrick and Hamrick's close friend Gary Martin had been notified. They arrived at the hospital at approximately 6:00 a.m. Johnston turned the chief's property over to Martin. He noted the time as 6:08 a.m. on his report. Martin confirmed this in his statement. He took the equipment, cleaned it up and gave everything to the family, except for the holster. The holster belonged to someone else, and Martin returned it to the owner, according to his report.

Doctors worked fast at Ashtabula General to administer emergency care to Hamrick but soon decided he needed more intensive care and should be transferred to the Cleveland Clinic. Hawkins Ambulance left with Hamrick for the Cleveland Clinic minutes later. Police cruisers ran interference and closed off the roads for the ambulance to pass into Cleveland.

Chapman began the accident investigation after the ambulance left the wreck for Ashtabula General Hospital. First, he checked the roadway between Route 45 and the accident scene for anything that could have caused Hamrick to lose control. He found nothing. Skid marks in the icy, loose gravel of the road indicated that Hamrick had lost control of his cruiser coming out of the curve 155 feet north of the tree that he struck. The tree was approximately 1 foot in diameter. The cruiser had bounced 3 feet off the tree after impact.

Austinburg Mobil Wrecker took the car to its station at the corner of Route 45 and Interstate 90, where it was secured. Chapman checked the car later and found Hamrick's personal effects in the back seat on the floor. He made an inventory, which included a policeman's service cap, a tear gas nightstick, a book of uniform citations, a long nightstick, a commercial band radio, a citizen band radio, a black attaché case, a flashlight emergency light with light and red flasher. When it was daylight, Chapman took photos of the crash scene.

After the ambulance left for the Cleveland Clinic, Johnston checked with Dispenza to get the registration on the car Hamrick was chasing. He learned it was a 1968 Javelin Rambler (not a Chevrolet) that belonged to a woman who lived in West Austinburg. At 7:00 a.m., he and Silva paid her a visit and

Chief Robert Hamrick was fatally injured when he missed a curve on Callender Road and struck a tree. *Ashtabula Sheriff's Department.*

found out she had left her car overnight at the Sunoco station on Route 45 and Interstate 90 to have it greased and oiled before moving to Florida the next day.

Johnston and two other deputies headed to the Sunoco station, where they found the attendant fixing a flat tire on the car in question. They thought that was suspicious. The attendant claimed that when he arrived at work that morning, the whitewall tire was flat and had marks on it that looked like it had been driven while nearly flat. The deputies thought the tire looked as though it had been "driven hard."

They found out the car had been parked outside with the keys in it all night. When they asked him what car he had driven the night before, he pointed to an older Rambler on the other side of the building. Johnston checked that car and found all the windows were covered with frost and the engine was cold.

Later that morning, the Javelin's owner met with sheriff's detective Harold S. Roach at the Sunoco station. She noticed her car had mud splashed along the sides and less than a quarter tank of gas. When she left it at the station the night before, it was clean and had three-quarters of a tank of gas.

Items that had been on the back shelf of her car were scattered on the back seat and floor, an indication that the car had made a sudden stop or had hit a bump in the road at a high rate of speed. The attendant claimed he had serviced the car, but there was no sticker on the door.

A brown filter-tip cigarette butt was lying on the front floor mat, but the owner did not smoke. Roach later noticed the station attendant smoking a cigarette with the same type of filter as the one in the car.

Patrolman Martin was already hearing the rumors that Hamrick had been pulled out of the car and beaten. He went to have a look for himself. "I checked the area, but could not find any indication of this," he wrote in his report. He also noted the ignition switch was bent, which indicated to him

The 1968 Dodge 4-door sedan (A-5) had severe damage to the front end. The engine was driven back toward the firewall. *Ashtabula Sheriff's Department.*

that it had been bumped into the off position on impact. Both the radio and emergency lights were off because they were wired to the ignition, he noted.

Hamrick was admitted to the Cleveland Clinic at 7:55 a.m. The attending physician noted he was comatose and had severe head injuries. He was operated on by and under the care of assistant neurosurgeon Dr. Moses Taghioff. In spite of everything that was done to save him, Robert Hamrick died at 5:15 p.m. on March 20 having never regained consciousness. An autopsy was performed the next day by Dr. Charles S. Hirsch. The coroner's verdict found: "The decedent came to his death as the result of: Blunt impact to head with contusion of brain and extensive brain swelling and necrosis." The report stated that his death was caused by the auto accident. However,

The steering wheel of Hamrick's cruiser (A-5) was driven out several inches. Hamrick's head hit the rear-view mirror. *Ashtabula Sheriff's Department.*

The driver's side door of the cruiser (A-5) was jammed shut. Hamrick was extracted through the passenger side door. *Ashtabula Sheriff's Department.*

a note that accompanied the coroner's request read, "Dr. Taghioff, who suspects foul play."

The note on the autopsy request made it plausible that Hamrick had been hauled out of his cruiser by Rock Creek Gang members, beaten and then put back in his cruiser—so did the blood on the ground outside the car and that someone had turned off the ignition and lights. It was also rumored that his gun and nightstick were missing. Rumors were spreading fast around Rock Creek, according to Mayor Schlecht in an incident report, so he asked then sheriff Tom Fasula to conduct an investigation.

Detective Terry Moisio wrote in a report on March 30 that Roach had learned from a "very good" informant that the station attendant was the driver of the car Hamrick was chasing. Martin said Hamrick had tried to stop the subject earlier in the evening but could not catch up to him. When Moisio went to look at the cruiser, he noted the severe damage. In particular, he found blood and hair on the rear-view mirror, as well as on the siren's control unit mounted on the dashboard and the CB radio mounted under the glove compartment. All of this indicated that Hamrick's head injuries happened during the accident.

Speculation and gossip died down over the years but never completely went away.

Unsolved Mysteries came to town in 1991 and featured family members. The sheriff's department turned over the Hamrick file to the filmmakers, and sheriff's deputies involved in the case, including Sheriff William Johnston, appeared on screen and cooperated fully. The show, which aired on November 20, did little to set things straight. Instead, it fueled the rumors that Hamrick had been murdered and "caused those rumors to increase," according to one of the sheriff's reports. The family persisted from day one in the idea that Hamrick had been murdered.

TeleTech Communications, responsible for receiving calls about *Unsolved Mysteries* segments, received about forty calls about the Hamrick case. Either Detective Joseph Foglio or Rock Creek police chief Keith Hopkins followed up on each call, but nothing of evidential value came out of the effort. Other calls came straight into the sheriff's department, but again, detectives learned nothing of value.

The family pressured Sheriff Johnston to reopen the case after *Unsolved Mysteries*, "Brenda's Fire," aired. In late 1991, investigators went back to work on the case. Detective Foglio sent the original medical file to Dr. Taghioff and asked about the note on the autopsy request that said he "suspects foul play." Taghioff wrote back to Foglio: "After very careful review of the files, I do not believe that there was any foul play involved. I feel that the cause of death was cerebral failure due to blunt impact to the head with contusions of the brain and extensive brain swelling and necrosis." He did not know why there was a note requesting the autopsy. He wrote that if he had thought there was foul play he would have noted it in the medical records.

Foglio wanted to know who wrote that note. A representative at the Cuyahoga County Coroner's Office named Dorothy pulled the file and saw the notation. She explained to Foglio that clerks filled out the intake forms and sometimes put their own opinion on the forms. At times, they would write "foul play" on the form where there was no foul play. Dorothy told the investigator that no one should pay attention to their notes.

In December 1991, Foglio requested the help of the Ohio State Highway Patrol Crash Reconstruction Unit to reconstruct the crash. Working with photos of Hamrick's cruiser, the autopsy report, a copy of the accident report, the detectives' and deputies' investigative reports and an Ashtabula County map, Lieutenant F.G. Goldstein, commander of crash reconstruction and analysis, wrote in a detailed letter how he concluded that Hamrick's injuries were consistent with the "severity and dynamics of the crash."

Above: Rock Creek police chief Robert Hamrick's grave site in Madison Memorial Cemetery in Madison, Lake County, Ohio. *Photo by Jane Ann Turzillo.*

Right: The Member of Fraternal Order of Police star is attached to Hamrick's tombstone. *Photo by Jane Ann Turzillo.*

In March 1992, Detectives Lawrence R. Eller III and Foglio went to New York City to see Dr. Charles S. Hirsch, who had performed Hamrick's autopsy while on staff at the Cuyahoga County Coroner's Office. Hirsch was a leading forensic medical examiner and the chief medical examiner for the City of New York. Before their meeting, Hirsch reviewed the report, which consisted of photographs taken during the autopsy and photos of the crashed cruiser, both interior and exterior. After a thorough review, he wrote in part to Eller, "Furthermore, there is no injury that suggests to me causation by assault with a blunt instrument such as a flashlight or night stick. Emphatically, the autopsy on Mr. Hamrick did not disclose evidence of multiple, discrete or separate impacts to his face and/or head." The doctor wrote that he would have easily detected injuries from foul play.

The Franklin County coroner, Dr. William R. Adrion, was also consulted. He wrote, "Reviewed autopsy record, and photography scene. Agree this is an auto accident death with no evidence to suggest prior beating with staged accident."

The Ohio Bureau of Criminal Investigation was also consulted and asked to look at the accident. Superintendent John Lenhart said that although the bureau found some conflicting statements, those statements did not place "reasonable doubt" on the investigations conducted by the sheriff's department, the coroners' reports and the Ohio State Highway Patrol. BCI's investigators believed that Hamrick died from the accident.

Sheriff Johnston closed the case in June 1992, but up until 1996, tipsters were still calling the sheriff's department claiming to have information on Hamrick's death. In 1995, two detectives met with an inmate at the Southern Ohio Correctional Facility in Lucasville who claimed to have information about Hamrick's death, but the convict only wanted help with getting a parole.

The same names kept cropping up, but they were given lie detector tests in late 1991 and early 1992 and passed them. One of them was the Sunoco station attendant. He admitted to taking the 1968 Javelin Rambler that night for a test-drive after working on its carburetor. While driving around town with his brother, he became the object of Hamrick's pursuit. He saw the chief's lights in his rear-view mirror. He sped up and got quite a bit ahead of Hamrick. After passing the bridge, he did not see Hamrick's lights anymore and assumed the chief had called off the chase. He wrote in his statement to detectives, "I'll have to live with it the rest of my life." Although Detective Roach was suspicious of him, he stated that he had "never been questioned by anyone at any time about the incident."

To this day, conspiracy theories are still bantered about on social news websites and forums. Even the Ohio Attorney General's website has Hamrick's death listed as an "unsolved homicide." At this writing, the Ohio Attorney General's Office has not responded to a Public Records Request.

Police Chief Robert G. Hamrick was laid to rest in the Madison Memorial Cemetery in Madison in Lake County. His story appears on the Officer Down Memorials page. On April 22, 1987, he posthumously received the Medal of Honor from the American Police Hall of Fame.

BIBLIOGRAPHY

Ancestry. ancestry.com.

And Then They Were Gone. "John and Shelly Markley." https://www. andthentheyweregone.com/blog/john-and-shelly-markley.

Ashtabula County Sheriff's Department File No. 70-1030. Sheriff Robert Hamrick accident and death, various incident reports, statements, investigation reports, accident reports, etc.

Biliczky, Carol. "Missing Police Chief Leaves Unsolved Mystery." *Akron Beacon Journal,* June 18, 2000.

Certificate of Death, Frederick Floyd Valentine, Oakland County, Michigan, May 26, 1941.

Certificate of Death, Indiana State Department of Health, Raymond C. Greenwood Sr., December 10, 1992.

Charley Project. "John J. Markley Jr." https://charleyproject.org/case/ john-j-markley-jr.

———. "Judy Martins." https://charleyproject.org/case/judy-martins.

———. "Shelly Renee Markley." https://charleyproject.org/case/shelly-renee-markley.

Coroner's Office, Cuyahoga County. Coroner's Verdict. Norman Lary Liver, Jr., Case No. 179100, October 17, 1980.

———. Coroner's Verdict. Robert Hamrick, Case No. 136094, March 21, 1970.

———. Coroner's Verdict. Unidentified White Female. Erie County, 0-80-12.

CourtTV. *The Unsolved Casefile.* "Cassidy Family Murder." May 13, 2021.

Divorce Record, Michigan Department of Health, Floyd A. Valentine from Eleanore Greenwood Valentine, November 1, 1943.

The Doe Network. "Johnny J. Markley." https://www.doenetwork.org/cases/2270dmoh.html.

Dugger, Brian. "Wearing her first pair of heels, she never made it home. Why there's new life in a 60-year cold case." WTOL, January 3, February 1, and February 16, 2023.

———. "Woman Found Dead on Sandusky Beach in 1980 Identified as Missing Michigan Woman." WTOL, April 4, 2023.

Edwards, Nik, and The Captain (Patrick Edwards). *True Crime Garage* podcast, episodes 607–610.

Erie County Sheriff Complaint Report, number not visible. 4-01-68, 4:02 AM.

Ferrise, Adam. "12-Year-Old Girl's Body Exhumed in 52-Year-Old Coventry Township Murder Case." Cleveland.com. November 14, 2014. https://www.cleveland.com/akron/2014/11/12-year-old_girls_body_exhumed.html.

Find a Grave. findagrave.com.

Fort Wayne, Indiana, Post-Mortem Examination. Nancy Eagleson, 60-A-177, November 14, 1960.

Glomerata vol. 46, Auburn University, 1943, p. 136.

Goldenberg, Sara. "Kent State Student Still Missing after 40 Years, Family Seeks Answers." 19 News. May 24, 2018. https://www.cleveland19.com/story/38274764/kent-state-student-still-missing-after-40-years-family-seeks-answers/.

Hendrickson, Dick. "Slain Couple's Son Energetic, Industrious Lad." *Morning Journal,* April 2, 1968.

Landers, Sheriff Jason K. "Nancy Eagleson Case." Email interview/questions, April 13, 2023.

Lane, Ellen Born. "Help with Questions on Norm Liver's Death." Email interview, July 2022.

Lucas County Coroner's Office. Autopsy report, Nancy Eagleson, A-1292-22, October 24, 2022.

Marriage License, Bay County, Michigan, Raymond Greenwood and Eleanore Kotewa, January 14, 1937.

Marriage License, Oakland County, Michigan, Floyd Adelbert Valentine and Eleanore Kotewa, April 3, 1940.

McKay, Bob. "The Case of the Vanishing Police Chief." *Cleveland Magazine,* October 1985.

Meyer, Richard. "More Than a Year Later, His Small Town Remains Baffled." *San Francisco Examiner*, December 14, 1986.

National Center for Missing & Exploited Children. www.missingkids.com.

O'Brien, Dave. "Mystery of Vanished KSU Student Spans 35 Years." *Record Courier*, May 26, 2013.

The Ohio Adult Parole Authority et al, Ohio State Reformatory Series 1522 BV5550.

Ohio Attorney General. "Missing Adult—Judy Martins." https://www.ohioattorneygeneral.gov/Files/Law-Enforcement/Investigator/Ohio-Missing-Persons/Missing-Adults-1/Martins.

Ohio State Reformatory Historical Code of Conduct p 1-64 (2 pages) for Robert Hamrick, prisoner no. 63051. Ohio History Connection Archives/Library microfilm GR6931.

O'Mara, Mike. "Hope Remains in 52-Year-Old Cold Case." WKYC, November 19, 2014.

Piorkowski, Jeff. "After 38 Years, Richmond Heights Police Have Teamed with Ohio BCI to Try to Find Frank Noch's Killers." Cleveland.com, August 5, 2022. https://www.cleveland.com/community/2022/08/after-38-years-richmond-heights-police-have-teamed-with-ohio-bci-to-try-and-find-resident-frank-nochs-killers.html.

Price, Mark. "Local History: Coventry Girl's Slaying Recalled on 50th Anniversary." *Akron Beacon Journal*, August 27, 2012.

Record Group 83-86, Department of Corrections, Administrative, Raymond Christopher Greenwood, Prisoner Index Cards, 1837–1987.

Record Group 96-164, Department of Corrections, State Prison of Southern Michigan, Raymond Christopher Greenwood, Prisoner Index Cards, 1870–1987.

Renner, James. "The Porchlight Project Will Fund Testing and Genetic Genealogy to Identify Erie County Jane Doe." Porchlight Project. November 29, 2021. https://porchlightonline.org/the-porchlight-project-to-fund-testing-and-genetic-genealogy-to-identify-erie-county-jane-doe/.

———. "The Porchlight Project Will Help Fund Exhumation of Nancy Eagleson." Porchlight Project. August 9, 2022. https://porchlightonline.org/the-porchlight-project-will-help-fund-exhumation-of-nancy-eagleson/.

Richmond Heights Police Department, Supplementary Report, Incident Number 84-1-0001, 2-20-84.

Sandusky Police Department, Investigative Report, INCD#:SPD-20-014411, 11/17/2020–3/30/2023.

Sandusky Police Department, Supplementary Report, No. 11, 3-30-80.

Schleis, Paula, and Stephanie Warsmith. "After Nearly 60 Years and an Exhumation, Coventry Girl's Murder Is Still a Mystery." *Akron Beacon Journal*, December 16, 2020.

———. "Detectives Hope DNA Tests Will Determine Who Killed Girl in 1962." *Daily Herald*, December 22, 2014.

Short, Michelle. "Mel Wiley: Did Ohio Police Chief Stage His Own Disappearance?" Crime Wire. June 3, 2023. https://thecrimewire. com/true-crime/mel-wiley-did-ohio-police-chief-stage-his-own-disappearance.

Siddiqi, Zahid H. "Records Request." Letter. Bureau of Criminal Investigation, August 3, 2023.

Summit County Sheriff's initial report (no case # visible). Marion Brubaker. Aug 27, 1962.

The Trail Went Cold. "John & Shelly Markley." ep. 316. https://www. trailwentcold.com/2023/02/15/the-trail-went-cold-episode-316-john-shclly-markley.

Trexler, Phil. "DNA Tests May Lead to Killer from 1962." *Akron Beacon Journal*, December 14, 2014.

Turzillo, Lucille. Diary entry, October 16, 1980.

Uncovered. "Justice Delayed: The Renewed Effort to Solved the Nancy Eagleson Case." February 16, 2023.

———. "Overview of Patricia Greenwood." April 4, 2023.

United States of America. Cleveland, Ohio District, Petition for Citizenship No. 44778, Frank Noch. Jan. 19, 1925.

Websleuths. "OH—Judy Martins, 22, Kent, 24 May 1978." https:// www.websleuths.com/forums/threads/oh-judy-martins-22-kent-24-may-1978.51675/.

Wendling, Ted. "Seamy Untold Story Surfaces in Hinckley Chief's Disappearance." *Plain Dealer*, July 28, 1991.

Winans, Carl W., D.O. Sandusky Memorial Hospital, Authorization for Autopsy, Erie County 0-80-12.

Windsor, Jeanne. Nancy Eagleson case, emails, March 3–April 12, 2023.

YouTube. "Eye on Justice: Unsolved: Cassidy Family Murders." March 17, 2021. https://www.youtube.com/watch?v=SeBetPsBpRs.

Zrilich, Joan. "Wiley Presumed a Run Away." *Hinckley Reporter* 28, no. 9, September 1985.

Newspapers

Akron Beacon Journal
Alliance Review
Canton Repository
Chillicothe Gazette (OH)
Cleveland Press
Cleveland Scene
Columbus Dispatch
Daily Jeffersonian (Cambridge, OH)
Delphos (OH) Courant
Detroit Free Press
Detroit Metro Times
Detroit News
Franklin (IN) Evening Star
Greensboro (AL) Watchman
Hinkley (OH) Reporter
Lima Citizen
Lima News
Morning Journal (Lorain, OH)
New-Messenger (Fremont, OH)
Paulding County Progress
Plain Dealer
Record-Courier (Kent Ravenna, OH)
Sandusky Register
Selma Times-Journal
South Bend (IN) Tribune
Traverse City (MI) Record Eagle
Time Recorder
Times Bulletin (VanWert, OH)
Tribune (Coshocton, OH)
Tribune Chronicle (Warren, OH)
21WFMJ, Nexstar Media, Inc. (Youngstown, OH)
27WKBN, Nexstar Media, Inc. (Youngstown, OH)
United Press International
Vindicator (Youngstown, OH)
Zanesville (OH) Times Recorder

ABOUT THE AUTHOR

J ane Ann Turzillo is a several-time National Federation of Press Women award winner and double Agatha Award nominee. She is a full-time author of ten books on Ohio history and true crime. As one of the original owners of a large weekly newspaper, she covered police and fire news. When she is not digging up history in old newspapers, police files, court records and cemeteries, she enjoys photography and playing with her German Shepherd, Doc Holliday, and her Border Collie mix, Pretty Boy Floyd. Visit her website at www. janeannturzillo.com and read her blog at http://darkheartedwomen.wordpress.com.

Photo by Elaine Copeland Curtis.

Visit us at
www.historypress.com